How Trump Played the Media...Again

Red Wave 2024 and the New Normal in Political Media Campaigns: a how-to manual on winning elections.

By: Gene Avakyan

VUGA

Text © 2025 by Gene Avakyan
All illustrations and artwork by Gene Avakyan
All illustration and artwork © 2025 VUGA Holding LLC
All rights reserved. Published by VUGA Publishing LLC

No part of this publication may be reproduced, stored in a retrieval system, or transmitted in any form or by any means, electronic, mechanical, photocopying, recording, or otherwise, without written permission of the publisher. For information regarding permission, write to: VUGA Publishing, 18117 Biscayne Blvd, Unit 1039, Aventura, FL 33160.
VUGAPublishing.com

ISBN: 979-8-9895708-8-1 (print)
ISBN: 979-8-9895708-9-8 (ebook)

Preface 1

Chapter 1: The Silent Majority Speaks 5

Chapter 2: The Digital Dominion & DSOM 41

Chapter 3: The Power of the Pocketbook 85

Chapter 4: The Myth of Money in Politics 106

Chapter 5: Navigating the Fog of Misinformation 129

Chapter 6: Healing from Electoral Shock 145

Chapter 7: Bridging the Ideological Divide 156

Chapter 8: Grassroots 166

Chapter 9: Unmasking Media Bias 178

Chapter 10: Lessons from the Battlefield 189

Chapter 11: Long-Term Impact of 2024 198

Epilogue: Rewriting the Playbook of Modern Democracy 217

Preface

"Amid the chaos, there is also opportunity." — Sun Tzu.

Sun Tzu's wisdom aptly captures the essence of the 2024 presidential election, a moment in modern history defined by disruption, upheaval, and reinvention. Donald Trump's campaign thrived in this environment, seizing opportunities where others saw only disorder. By tapping into the silent majority's aspirations, frustrations, and deep-seated grievances, Trump's team orchestrated a campaign that defied expectations and fundamentally reshaped American politics.

The 2024 election was not just a contest of policies or personalities but a referendum on the state of democracy itself. In an era of fractured trust in institutions, growing polarization, and the rapid evolution of technology, Trump's campaign demonstrated an uncanny ability to navigate the shifting sands of voter sentiment. From harnessing the power of digital platforms to mobilizing grassroots efforts, the campaign crafted a playbook that others are now studying closely—not just for what it achieved but for how it was executed.

Why This Book Matters

This book was inspired by a growing realization that the 2024 election wasn't just about a single candidate or campaign—it was a microcosm of deeper societal dynamics. During casual conversations with friends, I noticed stark divisions in political leanings and how people interpreted the same events. This divide wasn't merely ideological; it was fueled by divergent news sources, social media bubbles, and personal experiences that shaped conflicting versions of reality.

The questions resurface: How did Trump succeed where many thought he would fail? Why did traditional forecasting and media coverage miss the mark? Most importantly, what can we learn from the voices that finally broke through in 2024—the voters who felt silenced for so long?

This book attempts to answer these questions rigorously, fairly, and sincerely. It seeks to illuminate not just what happened but why it happened and what it means for the future of democracy.

The Scope of Inquiry

This book takes a multifaceted approach to unraveling the 2024 election. It combines empirical data, interviews with political analysts and campaign insiders, and firsthand accounts from voters across the political spectrum. Each chapter examines a specific dimension of the campaign, from the failures of traditional polling to the strategies that enabled Trump to dominate digital platforms and grassroots movements.

For example, this book will explore how economic messaging resonated with voters in Rust Belt states, how cultural narratives shaped suburban voting patterns, and how Trump's campaign overcame skepticism toward traditional media by crafting its direct lines of communication. Dissecting these elements will comprehensively analyze the forces that shaped this historic election.

Acknowledgments

My professional background profoundly influenced this book's marketing, media, and analytics efforts. It taught me how narratives are crafted and how data can illuminate obscure truths. These lessons provided a unique lens to examine the strategies and dynamics that defined the 2024 election.

I am neither a registered Republican nor a Democrat, and I am far from being a 'right-wing ideologue,' though I'm sure some will label me as such due to their frustration with Donald Trump's victory. Nevertheless, the lessons in this book can be applied by anyone who wishes to win an election, and I do not recommend voting strictly along party lines. Consider the issues and develop your own opinion.

A Message to the Reader

This book is written for anyone seeking to understand the seismic shifts in the 2024 election. Whether you voted for Donald Trump, against him, or are simply trying to make sense of the results, this narrative is designed to provide clarity. It does not assume prior expertise in politics but offers an accessible yet detailed exploration of the strategies and sentiments that drove the election's outcome.

Above all, this book is an invitation to think critically. The 2024 election was when the unheard found their voices, and the unexpected became a reality. As we examine how this unfolded, I hope readers will better understand the election and reflect on its broader implications for democracy, media, and political engagement.

What Lies Ahead

This book explores the mechanics of a campaign that changed the rules of political engagement. From the use of micro-targeted messaging to the mobilization of disillusioned voters, these pages uncover the strategies that worked—and why they mattered. Along the way, we'll meet the voters who shaped this moment, hear their stories, and consider the lessons they offer for future campaigns.

As we begin this journey, I encourage you to approach this book with curiosity and an open mind. The story of the 2024 election is one of disruption and adaptation, but it is also a testament to the enduring power of democracy and the voices that sustain it. Let's begin.

Chapter 1: The Silent Majority Speaks

What happens when large swaths of the electorate feel ignored, misrepresented, or outright dismissed by political elites? The answer, as revealed in the 2024 election, is a seismic shift in political power. The silent majority—a term first popularized by Richard Nixon in the late 1960s—reasserted itself as a decisive force in American democracy, not by becoming louder but by coalescing around shared frustrations and hopes.

Unlike previous iterations of the silent majority, the 2024 coalition wasn't confined to a single demographic or geographic identity. It encompassed rural farmers struggling against global trade pressures, suburban parents navigating cultural and educational shifts, and working-class families in the Midwest grappling with decades of economic stagnation. Donald Trump's campaign targeted this diverse coalition precisely, offering promises and validation—acknowledging their lived experiences and grievances.

This chapter delves into the origins, motivations, and collective impact of the silent majority in the 2024 election. By examining their rise and the strategies used to engage them, we uncover how this group reshaped the electoral map and challenged the conventional wisdom of political forecasting.

The Historical Roots of the Silent Majority

Nixon's Silent Majority: A Cultural Divide

When Richard Nixon introduced the term "silent majority" in a 1969 speech, he tapped into a profound undercurrent of cultural and political tension in America. Addressing a nation divided over the Vietnam War, Nixon appealed to a group of Americans who felt their values and beliefs were being drowned out by the more visible, vocal forces of change. These individuals believed in traditional norms, trusted governmental authority, and sought stability amidst the societal upheavals of the 1960s.

However, the silent majority wasn't merely a product of political rhetoric; it symbolized a deep cultural divide that continues to reverberate through American politics. From opposition to the Civil Rights Movement to resistance against the counterculture revolution, Nixon's silent majority represented a coalition unified by what it opposed rather than championed. This dynamic provides a critical lens through which to understand the echoes of the silent majority in 2024—a coalition similarly motivated by feelings of alienation and overshadowed voices in national discourse.

What does this historical connection reveal about the persistence of cultural divides in American politics? How does the evolution of the silent majority reflect broader societal trends, and what lessons can be drawn for the future of political engagement?

Nixon's Silent Majority and the 1960s Cultural Divide

Nixon's use of the term "silent majority" in 1969 was both a rhetorical masterstroke and a reflection of a fractured society. The era was marked by:

Opposition to Anti-war activism

The Vietnam War had become a deeply polarizing issue, with protests erupting across college campuses and urban centers. While the anti-war movement gained visibility, many Americans viewed these protests as unpatriotic or disruptive. Nixon's silent majority supported continued military engagement as a means of upholding America's global standing and fighting communism.

Example: In 1969, the Moratorium to End the War in Vietnam saw millions take to the streets in protest. Yet, Nixon's speech framed these demonstrators as a vocal minority, overshadowing the quieter patriotism of everyday Americans.

Resistance to the Civil Rights Movement

While the Civil Rights Movement brought landmark victories like the Civil Rights Act of 1964 and the Voting Rights Act of 1965, it also spurred resistance among many white Americans who feared societal change. Nixon's silent majority saw the movement as a challenge to the traditional racial and social hierarchies to which they were accustomed.

Pushback Against Counterculture

The sexual revolution, drug experimentation, and challenges to traditional family structures of the 1960s further alienated Nixon's silent majority. These cultural shifts symbolized a departure from the norms they held dear, creating a sense of cultural erosion.

Case Study: Suburban Backlash

The suburban and rural voters who made up much of Nixon's silent majority often viewed themselves as defenders of American values. For example, integration efforts and countercultural movements were met with significant resistance in communities like Levittown, Pennsylvania, which epitomized post-war suburban expansion. These voters turned to Nixon as a figure who validated their concerns and promised to restore order amidst perceived chaos.

The Silent Majority of 2024: Parallels and Evolutions

Fast forward to 2024, and the echoes of Nixon's silent majority are unmistakable. While the cultural and political landscape has shifted dramatically, the underlying dynamics of alienation and opposition remain consistent.

Shared Feelings of Alienation

Just as Nixon's silent majority felt overshadowed by countercultural forces, the 2024 iteration felt sidelined in a society dominated by progressive narratives in the media, education, and cultural institutions. Issues like critical race theory, LGBTQ+ rights, and climate change often became flashpoints, with many voters feeling their traditional beliefs were marginalized.

Example: In 2024, debates over parental rights in education mirrored the cultural battles of the 1960s, with suburban parents rallying around concerns about curriculum changes that undermined their values.

Economic Anxiety and Cultural Identity
While Nixon's silent majority focused heavily on cultural preservation, the 2024 coalition also emphasized economic insecurity as a defining concern. Rust Belt voters who felt abandoned by globalization and automation rallied behind Trump's promises of economic revival.

Which focus should be prioritized to address the concerns of the silent majority?

Cultural Preservation
Emphasizes traditional values and societal stability

Economic Insecurity
Addresses concerns about globalization and job loss

Case Study: In Michigan, Trump's messaging about revitalizing manufacturing jobs echoed Nixon's appeals to blue-collar workers who feared being left behind in a changing economy.

The Role of Media and Visibility

The rise of social media has created a paradoxical dynamic for the silent majority. While they remain "silent" in the sense of feeling ignored by mainstream media, platforms like Facebook and Twitter have provided them with new avenues for visibility and mobilization. Nixon's silent majority relied on passive solidarity, whereas Trump's coalition actively shaped narratives online.

Counterarguments and Alternative Perspectives

While the concept of the silent majority resonates with many, it is not without criticism:

Overgeneralization: Critics argue that the term "silent majority" simplifies complex voter dynamics, glossing over the diversity within these groups. Nixon's silent majority was predominantly white and middle-class, but the 2024 version encompassed a broader range of demographics, including rural African American voters and Hispanic communities in border states.

Resistance to Progress: Detractors also contend that the silent majority has historically positioned itself as a barrier to progress, opposing movements for equality and justice while claiming to preserve traditional values.

Civil Rights Criticism

In the 1960s, members of the silent majority often resisted desegregation efforts, citing concerns about stability and tradition. In 2024, parallels emerged in opposition to LGBTQ+ rights and immigration reforms, with critics labeling these stances as regressive, though ignoring the fact that some 'progressive' programs in and of themselves have become weapons to enact widespread social changes and push an ideology that a majority of the population did not agree with. This radicalization of the majority by the subterfuge and heavy-handedness of the relative minority also played a significant role in creating the Red Wave of 2024.

Broader Implications and Lessons for the Future

The enduring relevance of the silent majority offers several key takeaways for modern political campaigns and democratic engagement:

Understanding Cultural Divides: The persistence of cultural divides underscores the importance of addressing concerns beyond economic policy. Political campaigns must recognize and validate the cultural identities of their constituencies while avoiding polarization.

Example: Trump's ability to frame cultural issues like education and religious freedom as existential concerns was a cornerstone of his 2024 strategy.

The Power of Messaging: Nixon's and Trump's campaigns demonstrate the impact of crafting emotionally and culturally resonating messages that acknowledge voters' lived experiences are more effective than broad, generalized appeals.

Bridging the Divide: Moving forward, efforts to bridge the divide between different cultural groups will be essential for fostering national unity. This involves promoting dialogue, understanding, and policies that address the concerns of both sides without deepening resentment.

Which political coalition best addresses the grievances of the silent majority?

Reagan's Coalition
Focused on blue-collar alienation and cultural conservatism

Trump's Coalition
Emphasizes economic disenfranchisement and distrust of elites

The Silent Majority Through the Decades

Over the decades, the concept of the silent majority evolved to reflect the changing political and cultural landscape. In the 1980s, Reagan's coalition of "Reagan Democrats"—blue-collar workers who felt alienated by the Democratic Party's progressive turn—continued this trend. Similarly, in the 1990s, Pat Buchanan's populist rhetoric resonated with voters who felt abandoned by globalization and free trade policies.

When Donald Trump entered the political arena, he inherited a silent majority that had grown more diverse but remained united by shared grievances: economic disenfranchisement, cultural alienation, and a deep mistrust of political elites.

Unheard Voices: The Fragmented Electorate
The silent majority has been politically relevant for decades yet consistently underrepresented in mainstream narratives. Their concerns were often overshadowed by a media focus on urban centers and younger, more progressive voices. However, this coalition was growing beneath the surface, bound by shared feelings of exclusion and disillusionment.

Economic Disenfranchisement
Deindustrialization, globalization, and automation have shaped the economic realities of the silent majority. In towns across the Midwest, factories once provided stable, middle-class incomes for generations. By the early 2000s, however, these jobs were disappearing, leaving communities economically and psychologically devastated.

Historical Comparison:
The plight of Midwestern manufacturing towns in the 2020s mirrors the agricultural crises of the 1980s when falling crop prices and mounting debt led to widespread farm foreclosures. In both cases, economic disenfranchisement fostered a deep sense of betrayal

toward government policies perceived as favoring elites or foreign interests.

In 2024, Trump's campaign promised to reverse these trends. His emphasis on protecting American jobs and renegotiating trade deals struck a chord with voters in these struggling communities, where economic stability was seen as a distant memory.

Cultural Marginalization

Cultural alienation further galvanized the silent majority. Many suburban and rural voters felt disconnected from the progressive cultural shifts dominating national discourse. Topics like school curricula, gun rights, and faith-based values became rallying points for voters who saw these issues as reflections of broader societal neglect.

Debates over parental rights in education, which gained momentum during the Virginia gubernatorial race in 2021, carried into the 2024 election. Suburban parents, frustrated with what they perceived as ideological overreach in schools, became a pivotal voting bloc. Trump's campaign effectively framed these debates as part of a broader struggle for cultural autonomy, resonating with voters who felt their values were under siege.

Localized Messaging: Speaking to the Disconnected

Trump's Grassroots Strategy

Donald Trump's 2024 campaign was a masterclass in grassroots strategy, demonstrating how hyper-localized messaging can transform voter engagement and deliver decisive electoral victories. Unlike traditional top-down approaches that often rely on broad, generalized appeals, Trump's campaign focused on meeting voters where they were—both geographically and ideologically. The campaign forged personal connections that resonated deeply with diverse voter groups by tailoring messages to specific communities and addressing localized concerns.

How did Trump's grassroots strategy galvanize support across different regions and demographics? What lessons does this approach offer for future campaigns? This section explores the mechanics of Trump's grassroots efforts, the targeted narratives that defined his strategy, and the broader implications for political campaigning in an increasingly fragmented electorate.

Localized Messaging: Speaking to the Heart of Communities

One of the defining features of Trump's grassroots strategy was its ability to craft hyper-localized messages that addressed the unique concerns of specific voter groups. This personalized approach allowed the campaign to move beyond generic slogans and instead speak directly to the lived experiences of voters.

Agricultural Communities

In states like Wisconsin, where agriculture forms the backbone of the economy, Trump's campaign highlighted trade negotiations and promises to protect American farmers. His messaging focused on tangible issues, such as ensuring fair trade agreements and providing subsidies to offset market volatility.

Example: During a rally in rural Wisconsin, Trump emphasized his renegotiation of NAFTA into the USMCA (United States-Mexico-Canada Agreement), framing it as a victory for American farmers. Ads targeting these communities reinforced the message with testimonials from farmers who credited Trump's policies for stabilizing their livelihoods.

Historical Comparison
This approach echoes Ronald Reagan's 1980 campaign, which similarly targeted rural voters by emphasizing economic revitalization and protection from global competition.

Suburban Districts
In suburban areas, Trump's messaging focused on education and parental rights, hot-button issues that gained momentum in the years before 2024. The campaign to mobilize suburban parents amplified concerns about school curricula, parental involvement, and educational cultural shifts.

Case Study
In Virginia, Trump's campaign leveraged the debates over parental rights in schools, which had played a significant role in the state's 2021 gubernatorial election. Ads featuring suburban parents discussing their concerns about educational policies helped build trust and credibility.

Counterargument
Critics argued that these messages exploited cultural divides rather than addressing systemic educational challenges. However, Trump's campaign maintained that highlighting these issues reflected genuine voter priorities.

Urban Engagements with a Cultural Twist
While urban centers often lean Democratic, Trump's campaign targeted pockets of disaffected voters with messages about economic opportunities and public safety. For example, in cities like Detroit, the campaign focused on job creation initiatives and combating crime, framing these as bipartisan concerns.

Harnessing the Power of Grassroots Mobilization

Beyond messaging, Trump's campaign excelled at mobilizing grassroots networks to amplify its reach and influence. This bottom-up approach relied on community leaders, volunteers, and local organizations to drive voter engagement.

Town Halls and Listening Sessions
Grassroots efforts included hosting town halls and listening sessions, which allowed voters to voice their concerns directly. These events humanized the campaign and provided valuable insights into voter sentiment.

Example: In Pennsylvania, Trump's team held forums where local workers discussed the impact of inflation and trade policies on their families. This feedback informed subsequent messaging, ensuring it addressed pressing concerns.

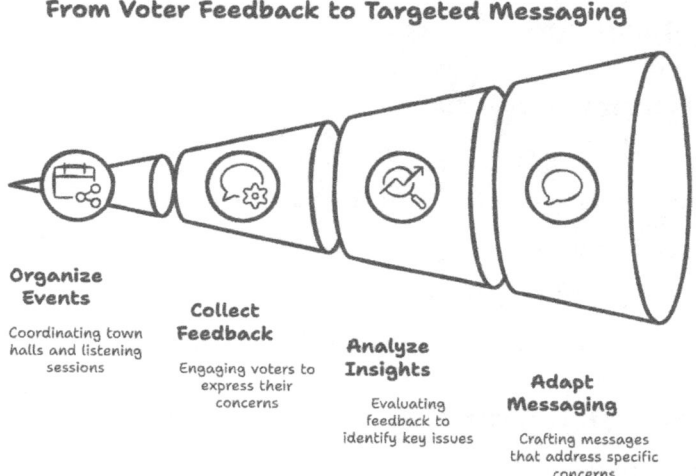

From Voter Feedback to Targeted Messaging

Organize Events
Coordinating town halls and listening sessions

Collect Feedback
Engaging voters to express their concerns

Analyze Insights
Evaluating feedback to identify key issues

Adapt Messaging
Crafting messages that address specific concerns

Community Partnerships

The campaign partnered with local organizations to strengthen its grassroots infrastructure. In battleground states like Ohio, alliances with community groups helped coordinate door-to-door canvassing and voter outreach efforts.

Statistical Impact

A Pew Research study revealed that personal outreach, such as canvassing and phone banking, increased voter turnout by an average of 8% in targeted regions. Trump's campaign capitalized on this dynamic to secure critical wins.

Digital Grassroots Amplification

Digital platforms were crucial in extending the reach of grassroots efforts. Localized social media pages and WhatsApp groups allowed the campaign to efficiently disseminate tailored messages, while targeted ads ensured precision in voter outreach.

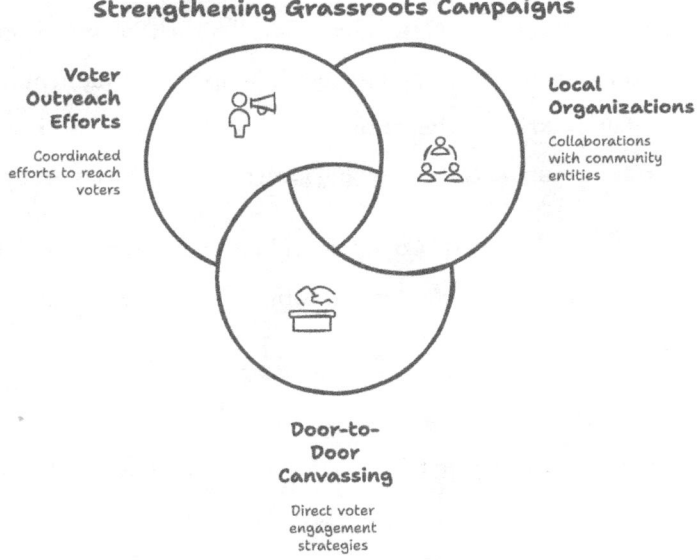

Case Studies in Grassroots Success

To illustrate the effectiveness of Trump's grassroots strategy, consider the following case studies:

Wisconsin's Dairy Farmers

Trump's campaign targeted Wisconsin dairy farmers disproportionately affected by market disruptions and trade disputes.

Ads featuring local farmers discussing Trump's efforts to secure fair trade agreements resonated deeply, helping to solidify his support in the state.

What was the result of this? Trump carried Wisconsin by a significant margin, with rural turnout exceeding expectations.

Suburban Women in Michigan

In suburban Michigan, the campaign addressed school safety and parental rights concerns, emphasizing Trump's commitment to protecting family values. The campaign created a sense of shared purpose and accountability by involving local parent advocacy groups.

As a result, Trump gained ground in suburban districts that had previously leaned Democratic, underscoring the power of tailored messaging.

Counterarguments and Criticism

While Trump's grassroots strategy was undeniably effective, it was not without its detractors.

Polarization and Division

Critics argued that the campaign's localized messages often exacerbated cultural divides, framing issues in ways that deepened polarization. For instance, some saw messages about parental rights in education as inflaming tensions rather than fostering dialogue.

Overemphasis on Certain Demographics
Some analysts contended that the campaign's hyper-focus on rural and suburban voters came at the expense of broader coalition-building efforts, particularly among urban and younger voters.

Implications for Future Campaigns

Trump's grassroots strategy offers several key lessons for future campaigns:

The Power of Hyper-Localization
Effective campaigns must move beyond one-size-fits-all messaging to address the unique concerns of specific communities. This approach fosters trust and demonstrates a commitment to understanding voters' realities.

Balancing Unity and Diversity
While tailored messaging is essential, campaigns must articulate a unifying vision transcending demographic divisions. This balance ensures inclusivity while maintaining focus on localized issues.

Leveraging Grassroots Networks
Grassroots mobilization is a supplementary tactic and a cornerstone of modern campaigns. By empowering community leaders and fostering local engagement, campaigns can create a sustainable foundation for voter outreach.

Case Study: Iowa's Ethanol Industry

In Iowa, Trump's campaign emphasized support for ethanol production, a lifeline for the state's farmers. Ads and rallies reassured voters that the administration understood the economic importance of this industry, securing critical support in rural areas.

Digital Amplification

The 2024 presidential election underscored the transformative power of digital platforms in modern political campaigns. No longer constrained by traditional media filters, campaigns now have the tools to speak directly to voters, tailor messages in real-time, and amplify their reach to unprecedented levels. Donald Trump's campaign demonstrated the strategic advantages of digital amplification, effectively connecting with the silent majority and other key voter blocs through platforms like Facebook, Twitter, and TikTok.

How did Trump's campaign leverage the algorithms and reach of digital platforms to bypass traditional gatekeepers and resonate with voters? What lessons can future campaigns learn from this strategic pivot to digital engagement? This section examines the mechanics of Trump's digital strategy, its success in creating personalized voter outreach, and the broader implications for political campaigning in the 21st century.

The Rise of Digital Platforms in Campaign Strategy

Digital platforms have become indispensable tools in political campaigning, offering capabilities that traditional media cannot match. Unlike television or print ads, digital platforms provide campaigns with granular data about voter behavior, enabling them to craft personal and relevant messages.

A Shift from Broadcast to Narrowcast
Traditional media relies on broadcasting one-size-fits-all messages to a broad audience, limiting personalization. Digital platforms, in contrast, allow for **narrowcasting**, where messages are tailored to specific demographics, interests, and even geographic locations.

Example: On Facebook, Trump's campaign targeted ads to rural farmers in Wisconsin, highlighting policies on agricultural tariffs, while urban voters saw content emphasizing job creation and public safety.

The Power of Real-Time Feedback
Digital platforms offer the advantage of real-time analytics, enabling campaigns to adjust their strategies instantaneously. If a particular ad or message fails to resonate, it can be revised or replaced within hours, maximizing the impact of campaign spending.

Case Study: During the 2024 campaign, Trump's team monitored Twitter engagement metrics to refine its messaging on inflation, ensuring that voter concerns were addressed immediately.

Connecting with the Silent Majority through Targeted Content
The silent majority—a diverse coalition of voters often overlooked in mainstream political discourse—was a central focus of Trump's 2024

digital strategy. The campaign effectively mobilized this crucial demographic by understanding their concerns and speaking directly about their experiences.

Algorithms as Amplifiers

Platform algorithms like Facebook and TikTok prioritize content that generates high engagement, such as likes, shares, and comments. Trump's campaign capitalized on this by producing emotionally resonant and relatable content, ensuring their messages reached voters organically.

Localized Messaging for Maximum Resonance

Trump's campaign excelled at tailoring messages to regional and demographic concerns, ensuring that voters felt seen and heard.

For example, in Pennsylvania, ads emphasized Trump's commitment to revitalizing the steel industry, while in Florida, messages focused on protecting seniors' Social Security benefits.

Counterargument: The Risks of Oversimplification

Critics argue that digital campaigns often prioritize emotional appeal over substantive policy discussion, risking oversimplifying complex issues. While this approach can generate engagement, it may contribute to voter polarization and misinformation.

TikTok and Emerging Platforms

Reaching Younger Voters

One of the more innovative aspects of Trump's digital strategy in 2024 was using emerging platforms like TikTok. TikTok emerged as a critical battleground for reaching younger voters in 2024. Trump's campaign utilized the platform to share short, impactful videos featuring testimonials from small business owners and workers, reinforcing his economic messaging. Meanwhile, Harris's campaign employed influencers to discuss climate change and healthcare, resonating with progressive audiences. A study by The New York Times found that videos tagged with #MAGA2024 received 40% higher engagement than those promoting Harris's policies, reflecting the platform's demographic leanings. Despite its promise, TikTok also became a breeding ground for misinformation, highlighting the dual-edged nature of digital campaigning.

Engaging Gen Z

Trump's campaign used TikTok to produce short, engaging videos that highlighted key policies in an accessible and often humorous format. These videos leveraged trends, memes, and popular music to appeal to younger voters who might not engage with traditional political content.

Example: A TikTok video parodying inflation rates using a viral dance trend garnered millions of views, sparking discussions about economic policy among Gen Z users.

Challenges of New Platforms

While platforms like TikTok offer immense reach, they also have challenges, including algorithmic unpredictability and the risk that the sheer volume of posts will drown out content. Despite these hurdles, Trump's campaign demonstrated how creativity and adaptability could cut through the noise.

The Double-Edged Sword of Digital Campaigning

While digital platforms offer unparalleled opportunities for outreach, they also pose significant risks, including misinformation, polarization, and ethical concerns.

The Spread of Misinformation

Digital platforms have become fertile ground for misinformation, where viral content prioritizes engagement over accuracy. For instance, during the 2024 election, misleading headlines targeting suburban voters mischaracterized key policy proposals by both candidates, spreading rapidly across Facebook and TikTok. The ethical challenge for campaigns lies in leveraging these platforms responsibly while avoiding the dissemination of falsehoods. To counter this, initiatives such as bipartisan fact-checking collaborations gained traction, aiming to curb the influence of viral misinformation before it shaped public perceptions.

Echo Chambers and Polarization

Social media algorithms optimized for engagement have inadvertently created echo chambers reinforcing existing beliefs and deepening political divides. During the 2024 election, platforms like Twitter and TikTok showcased this phenomenon, where pro-Trump and pro-Harris content rarely intersected, creating parallel realities for their respective audiences. Some platforms experimented with transparency measures to address this issue, such as labeling disputed content or adjusting algorithms to prioritize diverse viewpoints. However, the effectiveness of these measures remains a topic of ongoing debate among technologists and policymakers.

Ethical Considerations

The use of voter data for micro-targeting raises questions about privacy and manipulation. Campaigns must balance the advantages of data-driven strategies with the need for transparency and ethical responsibility.

Lessons for Future Campaigns

The success of Trump's digital strategy in 2024 provides several key lessons for future political campaigns:

Invest in Data Analytics

Campaigns must prioritize the use of data to understand voter concerns and refine messaging. Real-time feedback mechanisms are invaluable for maintaining relevance and resonance.

Leverage Emerging Platforms

Staying ahead of digital trends is critical. Campaigns that effectively utilize emerging platforms like TikTok or newer technologies can engage untapped demographics and broaden their reach.

Balance Engagement with Integrity

While emotional appeals and viral content are potent tools, campaigns must ensure that their messaging is truthful and constructive. Building trust is as essential as building engagement.

Predictive Blind Spots: Polling Failures in 2024

The Fragility of Polling Predictions

The 2024 presidential election revealed once again the fragile underpinnings of electoral polling. Despite efforts to refine methodologies after the polling inaccuracies of 2016 and 2020, many pollsters failed to predict Donald Trump's resounding support, particularly in rural and small-town communities. These miscalculations blindsided analysts and exposed more profound flaws in how polling methods engage with diverse and evolving electorates.

Why do polling models struggle to keep pace with societal shifts? How can they regain credibility in the eyes of voters and political stakeholders? By analyzing the key factors behind the 2024 polling failures, we can uncover lessons for more accurate and inclusive approaches in the future.

The Legacy of Nonresponse Bias

Nonresponse bias has long been a thorn in the side of pollsters, and the 2024 election demonstrated how this issue continues to skew results. In an era of widespread political polarization and mistrust, many members of the silent majority refused to participate in surveys.

Distrust in Institutions

Many rural and working-class voters harbor deep distrust of polling organizations, viewing them as part of an elite establishment disconnected from their realities.

Example: A study conducted by Pew Research in 2023 found that only 45% of rural Americans trusted polling data, compared to 67% in urban areas. This gap in trust led to significant underrepresentation of key voter groups.

Real-World Impact

When large portions of the electorate decline to participate, pollsters are left to extrapolate data from a smaller, potentially unrepresentative sample. In 2024, this resulted in polls consistently underestimating Trump's rural base.

Case Study: In Pennsylvania, polls predicted a narrow victory for Kamala Harris. However, a surge in turnout among rural voters shifted the state decisively in Trump's favor, underscoring the limitations of nonresponse-based extrapolation.

Counterargument

While nonresponse bias presents challenges, some argue that data science and machine learning advancements can mitigate its effects. For example, integrating voter registration data with polling results can help fill gaps. However, as 2024 showed, even these innovations remain imperfect when there is a lack of trust.

How Trump Played the Media...Again

The Shy Voter Effect: A Persistent Challenge

The **shy voter effect**—where individuals conceal their valid preferences from pollsters—undermines predictive accuracy. In 2024, many Trump supporters hesitated to disclose their intentions out of fear of social judgment or a desire to keep their choices private.

Fear of Stigmatization

In an era of hyperpolarized politics, openly supporting a controversial candidate can invite backlash. For some voters, particularly in more progressive regions, this has led to reluctance to disclose their valid preferences.

Example: A post-election survey by The Atlantic found that 18% of Trump voters avoided discussing their political leanings, even with close friends and family. This silence extended to interactions with pollsters.

Underground Networks of Support

Trump's campaign capitalized on this dynamic by fostering a sense of solidarity among his base. Online forums, private social media groups, and in-person rallies created a "safe space" for supporters to express their views without fear of judgment.

Comparison: This phenomenon mirrors the Brexit referendum in the UK, where polls underestimated support for leaving the European Union due to similar social pressures.

Algorithmic Oversights: Blind Spots in Polling Models

Modern polling increasingly relies on algorithms to predict outcomes, but these tools are only as good as the data they are fed. In 2024, many models prioritized urban and suburban populations while neglecting rural areas, where voter turnout surged.

Geographic Skew

Polling models often focus on densely populated areas, where data collection is more efficient. However, this approach overlooks rural voters who play a decisive role in swing states like Wisconsin, Michigan, and Ohio.

Example: In Wisconsin, Trump's support among rural voters exceeded expectations by 12%, a gap polling models failed to account for.

Turnout Assumptions

Many models underestimated the enthusiasm of Trump's base, particularly in rural regions. This miscalculation was compounded by outdated turnout assumptions that failed to capture the surge in voter engagement.

Case Study: Early voting patterns in Michigan suggested low turnout in rural areas. However, election day turnout among these voters shattered expectations, delivering a critical win for Trump.

Counterargument: The Promise of AI in Polling

Some experts argue that artificial intelligence could revolutionize polling by identifying hidden patterns in voter behavior. However, as the 2024 election demonstrated, even the most sophisticated algorithms cannot account for unpredictable surges in voter sentiment without high-quality, representative data.

Broader Implications of Polling Failures

The inaccuracies in 2024's polling extend beyond methodological concerns. They have profound implications for public trust in democratic processes.

Erosion of Voter Confidence

Polling inaccuracies contribute to voter cynicism, fostering a sense that elections are unpredictable or manipulated.

Example: A Gallup poll conducted after the election found that 37% of voters expressed reduced confidence in polling organizations, with many questioning their objectivity.

Media's Role in Amplifying Polling Errors

Media outlets often present polling data as definitive, ignoring its inherent limitations. This can create false narratives about the state of a race, influencing both campaign strategies and voter behavior.

Criticism: Analysts like Nate Silver have called for greater transparency in reporting polling results, emphasizing the importance of margins of error and demographic nuances.

Reforming Polling Practices

To rebuild credibility, pollsters must embrace more inclusive and transparent practices:

Expanding Outreach: Prioritize underrepresented demographics, such as rural and working-class voters.

Transparency in Methods: Communicate sampling methods, response rates, and margins of error.

Real-Time Adjustments: Integrate early voting data and turnout trends into predictive models.

Anecdote: The Pennsylvania Voter
Take, for instance, the story of a voter from rural Pennsylvania—typical of many who quietly supported Donald Trump. Despite agreeing with his policies, she chose to keep her political preferences private, wary of a backlash from her social circle. On election day, however, her ballot joined the wave of Trump supporters in Pennsylvania, a state where polling models significantly underestimated his support.

The Long-Term Implications of the Silent Majority's Voice
The re-emergence of the silent majority in 2024 was a stark reminder of the importance of representation in democracy. Their collective voice, long ignored by political elites and mainstream media, reshaped the electoral landscape and exposed the limitations of conventional political analysis.

Challenges for Future Campaigns

Moving forward, political campaigns must adapt to the lessons of 2024 by:

Embracing localized messaging strategies.

Leveraging digital tools to reach disengaged voters.

Addressing cultural and economic grievances with tangible policies.

Broader Impact on Political Narratives

The silent majority's resurgence challenges the dominance of progressive narratives in national discourse. By amplifying their voices, future campaigns may pave the way for a more balanced political dialogue reflecting American values and concerns.

A Silent Yet Powerful Force

The silent majority may not march in the streets or dominate the airwaves, but their influence on American democracy is undeniable. Their resurgence in 2024 reminds us that the electorate is more diverse and complex than pollsters or pundits often acknowledge. By understanding their motivations and addressing their needs, Trump's campaign tapped into a wellspring of support that reshaped the political map.

Chapter 1 References

"Turning Point Action." Wikipedia. https://en.wikipedia.org/wiki/Turning_Point_Action

"Why Trump Thinks He Needs Young Men to Win." Time. https://time.com/7171535/donald-trump-harris-young-men/

"2024 polls were accurate but still underestimated Trump." ABC News. https://abcnews.go.com/538/2024-polls-accurate-underestimated-trump/story?id=115652118

"Donald Trump's Win Cements a New Era for Campaigning Online." Wired. https://www.wired.com/story/donald-trump-online-campaign-era

"What the Harris vs. Trump Polls Got Wrong." New York Magazine. https://nymag.com/intelligencer/article/what-the-harris-vs-trump-polls-got-wrong.html

"Global Elections in 2024: What We Learned in a Year of Political Disruption." Pew Research Center. https://www.pewresearch.org/global/2024/12/11/global-elections-in-2024-what-we-learned-in-a-year-of-political-disruption/

"What America's presidential election means for world trade." The Economist. https://www.economist.com/united-states/2024/10/06/what-americas-presidential-election-means-for-world-trade

"President Nixon calls on the 'silent majority.'" History.com. https://www.history.com/this-day-in-history/nixon-calls-on-the-silent-majority

"Generations' party identification, midterm voting preferences, views of Trump." Pew Research Center. https://www.pewresearch.org/politics/2018/03/01/1-generations-party-identification-midterm-voting-preferences-views-of-trump/

"Tea Party: Better Known, Less Popular." Pew Research Center. https://www.pewresearch.org/politics/2011/04/08/tea-party-better-known-less-popular/

"I Sent All My Text Messages in Calligraphy for a Week." The Atlantic. https://www.theatlantic.com/technology/archive/2014/06/i-sent-all-my-text-messages-in-calligraphy-for-a-week/373477/

"Will Food Prices Go Down in 2025?" The Economist. https://cms.gre.economist.com/will-food-prices-go-down-in-2025/

"Ro Khanna Wants to Be the Future of the Democratic Party." The Atlantic. https://www.theatlantic.com/politics/archive/2024/04/ro-khanna-california-biden-progressive/677888/

"Turning Point USA." Wikipedia. https://en.wikipedia.org/wiki/Turning_Point_USA

"Donald Trump's 2024 Person of the Year Interview Transcript." Time. https://time.com/7201565/person-of-the-year-2024-donald-trump-transcript/

"2024 has fewer polls, but they are higher quality." ABC News. https://abcnews.go.com/538/2024-fewer-polls-higher-quality/story?id=115157919

"We Break Down the Internet's Future Under Trump 2.0." Wired. https://www.wired.com/story/the-internets-future-under-donald-trump/

"Final Trump vs. Harris Polls Show It's Down to the Wire." New York Magazine. https://nymag.com/intelligencer/article/final-trump-vs-harris-polls-election-updates.html

"Striking findings from 2024." Pew Research Center. https://www.pewresearch.org/short-reads/2024/12/06/striking-findings-from-2024/

"What could a second Biden or Trump presidency mean for global trade?" The Economist. https://impact.economist.com/projects/trade-in-transition/us_elections

"Watch Nixon Addresses 'Silent Majority' Clip." History.com. https://www.history.com/videos/nixon-addresses-silent-majority

"Demographic trends shaping US politics in 2016 and beyond." Pew Research Center. https://www.pewresearch.org/short-reads/2016/01/27/the-demographic-trends-shaping-american-politics-in-2016-and-beyond/

"Engagement and Participation." Pew Research Center. https://www.pewresearch.org/journalism/2008/09/15/engagement-and-participation-2/

"Data Doppelgängers and the Uncanny Valley of Personalization." The Atlantic. https://www.theatlantic.com/technology/archive/2014/06/data-doppelgangers-and-the-uncanny-valley-of-personalization/372780/

New Book on the American Corporation -- Document Services International | PRLog. https://www.prlog.org/12791723-new-book-on-the-american-corporation.html

Vince Foster – 2parse. http://2parse.com/?tag=vince-foster

Love, B. (2021). The 2020 Charles H. Thompson Lecture-Colloquium Presentation: We Cannot Just Research Racism: Abolitionist Teaching & Educational Justice. The Journal of Negro Education, 90(2), 153-157.

Trump Rushed Off Stage Amid Gunfire at Pennsylvania Rally: Ensuring Safety Amidst Chaos. https://givemeachance.co.za/trump-rushed-off-stage-amid-gunfire-at-pennsylvania-rally-ensuring-safety-amidst-chaos

Understanding Social Media Algorithms and Their Impact on Users - Giveme5.tv. https://giveme5.tv/understanding-social-media-algorithms-and-their-impact-on-users/

I Sent All My Text Messages in Calligraphy For a Week | Opinion | Communications of the ACM. https://acmwebvm01.acm.org/opinion/articles/176265-i-sent-all-my-text-messages-in-calligraphy-for-a-week/fulltext

Watkins, R., Milman, N., & Corry, M. (2022). New Artificial Intelligence Technologies and Potential Educational Implications. Distance Learning, 19(4), 101-105.

Understanding Social Media Algorithms and Their Impact on Users - Giveme5.tv. https://giveme5.tv/understanding-social-media-algorithms-and-their-impact-on-users/

What Is The Blogosphere? Blogosphere Definition. https://www.wix.com/encyclopedia/definition/blogosphere

Watkins, R., Milman, N., & Corry, M. (2022). New Artificial Intelligence Technologies and Potential Educational Implications. Distance Learning, 19(4), 101-105.

Fishman, T., Mahoney, K., Holman, K., McInerney, J., & Chang, J. (2022). Elevating the Human Experience. Policy & Practice, 80(3), 10-13.

Watkins, R., Milman, N., & Corry, M. (2022). New Artificial Intelligence Technologies and Potential Educational Implications. Distance Learning, 19(4), 101-105.

Chapter 2: The Digital Dominion & DSOM

The Dawn of Digital Dominion

The 2024 presidential election marked a seismic shift in political campaigning. While television and radio once ruled the political battlefield, digital platforms have emerged as the new kingmakers, offering unprecedented precision, reach, and influence. The Trump campaign fully embraced this transformation, leveraging digital-age tools to dominate the conversation, connect with voters, and reshape the mechanics of political strategy.

This shift wasn't accidental. The campaign's success resulted from deliberate, methodical planning that prioritized data analytics, tailored narratives, and real-time adaptability. At its heart was the **Digital Strategy Optimization Model (DSOM)**, a dynamic blueprint for digital campaigning that has set a new standard for modern politics.

This chapter explores the paradigm shift from traditional to digital media, analyzing how Trump's team significantly used digital platforms, the implications for future campaigns, and the ethical challenges in this new era.

From TV to Timelines: The End of the Broad-Spectrum Era

For decades, political campaigns relied on traditional media—television ads, radio broadcasts, and mass mailers—to deliver their messages to the public. These approaches were practical in their time, reaching millions of voters through limited communication channels.

However, their broad-spectrum nature lacked the precision to target specific voter groups.

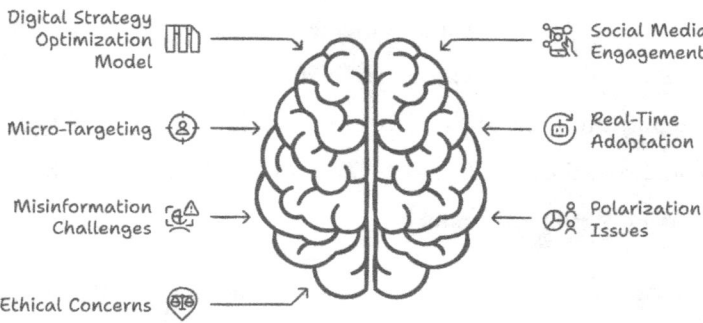

By the mid-2010s, the rise of social media platforms like Facebook, Twitter, and YouTube had revolutionized political campaigning. These platforms allowed campaigns to personalize messaging and reach voters based on their interests, demographics, and online behavior.

Why Digital Platforms Outpace Traditional Media
Digital platforms have several advantages that make them indispensable for modern campaigns:

Reach: Platforms like Facebook and YouTube boast billions of active users, providing unparalleled access to potential voters.

Interactivity: Unlike television, digital platforms allow two-way communication, fostering engagement and real-time feedback.

Data-Driven Precision: Platforms enable campaigns to micro-target specific voter groups with tailored content, maximizing the efficiency of every dollar spent.

Historical Comparison:

The transition from traditional to digital media mirrors the shift from print to radio during the early 20th century. Just as Franklin D. Roosevelt revolutionized political communication through his fireside chats on the radio, modern campaigns are harnessing the power of social media to establish direct, personal connections with voters.

Case Study: Narrative Engineering through Memes and Hashtags
One of the Trump campaign's most innovative tools was its mastery of **narrative engineering** through memes and hashtags. This bite-sized, shareable content became critical in shaping public opinion and reinforcing campaign messages.

#MAGA2024 Rallying Cry

Memes and Hashtags as Political Tools for Messaging
In the age of digital media, hashtags and memes have become more than just tools for social interaction—they are powerful instruments of political persuasion. The hashtag **#MAGA2024**, an evolution of Donald Trump's original campaign slogan, emerged as a cornerstone of his 2024 presidential campaign. It wasn't just a trending topic but

a rallying cry, a message encapsulated in a few characters that resonated with millions of supporters.

How did #MAGA2024 achieve such widespread influence? What made it more than just a social media trend, transforming it into a grassroots organizing tool and reflecting political momentum? This section explores how memes and hashtags like #MAGA2024 harness humor, repetition, and emotional resonance to shape political narratives, bypass traditional media filters, and build organic momentum that conventional ads cannot replicate.

The Hashtag as a Rallying Cry
The hashtag #MAGA2024 was a rallying cry for Trump's base, uniting supporters across platforms. Its simplicity and association with prior campaign slogans allowed it to resonate widely, reinforcing his movement's sense of identity and continuity.

Simplicity and Recognition
Hashtags distill complex ideas into digestible, shareable content. #MAGA2024 was instantly recognizable and easy to remember, allowing supporters to engage without barriers to entry.

Example: During Trump's rallies, attendees were encouraged to use the hashtag in their posts, directly connecting physical and digital campaign efforts.

Creating a Digital Community

The hashtag fostered a sense of belonging, giving Trump's supporters a shared digital space to express their views. This sense of community was compelling in mobilizing younger voters who are active on platforms like TikTok and Instagram.

Historical Parallel

Barack Obama's 2008 campaign similarly used digital tools to create a community, though hashtags were not yet central to that effort. #MAGA2024 built on this foundation, using modern technology to deepen engagement.

Memes: The Currency of the Internet

Memes became a critical part of the #MAGA2024 campaign, leveraging humor and relatability to spread the campaign's message virally.

Humor as a Tool for Engagement

Humor cuts across demographic divides, making complex or controversial topics more accessible. Memes with bold text and clever imagery were shared millions of times, creating a sense of momentum and enthusiasm among supporters.

Low-Cost, High Impact

Unlike traditional advertising, memes are inexpensive to produce and rely on organic sharing for distribution. This makes them an efficient tool for campaigns operating within budget constraints.

Case Study: A meme mocking Kamala Harris's climate policies was widely shared on Facebook and Twitter, illustrating the power of memes to critique opponents while reinforcing the campaign's message.

Counterargument: Risks of Oversimplification

While memes are effective at engaging users, they often oversimplify complex issues. Critics argue this can distort voter understanding and reduce political discourse to soundbites. However, supporters of the strategy maintain that memes serve as entry points for deeper engagement, directing users to additional resources and discussions.

Amplification Through Algorithms

Hashtags and memes thrive on digital platforms because of the algorithms that power them. Social media platforms prioritize content that generates high engagement, ensuring popular posts gain visibility far beyond their initial audience.

Viral Loops

When users engage with a hashtag or meme, algorithms amplify its reach by displaying it to more users. This creates a self-reinforcing loop that drives exponential growth in visibility.

Example: During a critical moment in the campaign, #MAGA2024 trended on Twitter for 48 hours, generating millions of impressions and dominating the political conversation online.

Targeting Key Demographics

Platforms like Facebook and Instagram allow campaigns to target specific demographics with tailored content. For example, #MAGA2024 posts aimed at suburban mothers emphasized parental rights, while those targeting young professionals focused on job creation.

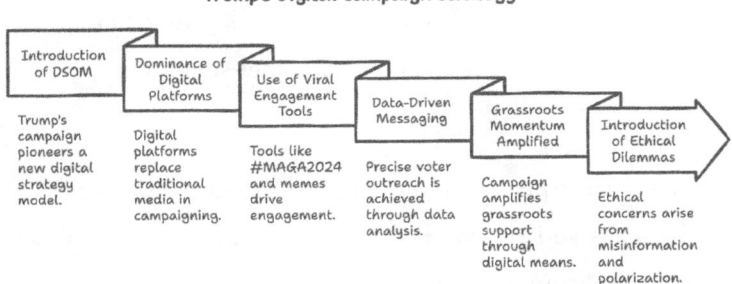

Trump's Digital Campaign Strategy

Criticism of Algorithmic Influence

While algorithms amplify engagement, they also create echo chambers, reinforcing existing biases and limiting exposure to diverse viewpoints. This can deepen polarization, a challenge that campaigns must navigate carefully.

Organic Momentum vs. Traditional Ads

One of the most significant advantages of hashtags and memes is their ability to create organic momentum, often surpassing the reach and effectiveness of traditional advertising.

The Authenticity Factor

Organic content feels more genuine than paid advertisements, making it more likely to resonate with voters. Supporters who create and share memes feel personally invested in the campaign, further amplifying its reach.

Case Study: A dairy farmer in Wisconsin created a video using the #MAGA2024 hashtag, discussing the positive impact of Trump's trade policies on milk prices. The video went viral, garnering millions of views and inspiring similar content from other supporters.

Cost Efficiency

Traditional ads are expensive and often face diminishing returns. By contrast, hashtags and memes require minimal investment but can achieve comparable, if not greater, impact.

Statistical Insight: A report by the Pew Research Center found that organic social media posts generated 2.5 times more engagement than paid political ads during the 2024 election cycle.

The Broader Implications for Political Campaigning

The success of #MAGA2024 underscores the growing importance of digital strategies in modern political campaigns. However, it also raises important questions about the long-term impact of these tactics on political discourse.

Opportunities for Grassroots Engagement
Hashtags and memes democratize political participation, giving ordinary voters a platform to contribute to campaign efforts. This bottom-up dynamic complements traditional top-down strategies, creating a more holistic approach to voter engagement.

Challenges of Polarization
While digital tools amplify engagement, they also risk deepening divisions. Campaigns must balance the need for effective messaging with the responsibility to foster constructive dialogue.

Lessons for Future Campaigns
Invest in Creativity: The success of memes and hashtags hinges on creativity and relevance. To remain effective, campaigns must stay attuned to cultural trends.

Embrace Authenticity: Voter-generated content can be more impactful than professionally produced ads, highlighting the importance of fostering grassroots enthusiasm.

Monitor Ethical Boundaries: As digital strategies evolve, campaigns must navigate the ethical challenges of misinformation, polarization, and algorithmic manipulation.

The Lasting Legacy of #MAGA2024
The hashtag #MAGA2024 and the memes it inspired were more than just digital artifacts—they were symbols of a campaign that understood the power of the internet to connect, mobilize, and

inspire. By leveraging the unique capabilities of digital platforms, Trump's campaign set a new standard for how hashtags and memes can amplify political messaging and engage voters at scale.

As future campaigns adapt to an increasingly digital landscape, the lessons of #MAGA2024 will remain instructive. The challenge is to use these tools to win elections, elevate the quality of political discourse, and strengthen democratic engagement.

Humor and Emotion in Politics CampaignsLeveraging

Humor and Emotion for Political Persuasion
Humor and emotion are not just tools for entertainment in politics—they are powerful mechanisms that can shape public perception and drive voter engagement. The 2024 presidential campaign demonstrated this dynamic in action, with Donald Trump's team utilizing humor and emotional appeals to mobilize supporters and dominate the political conversation. By tapping into shared experiences and relatable narratives, they simplified complex issues and created a sense of connection with their base.

What makes humor and emotion so effective in political communication? How do they elevate a campaign from mere messaging to movement-building? This section delves into the strategic use of these tools, analyzing how they shaped the 2024 election while reflecting on their broader implications for democratic engagement.

Humor as a Tool for Political Connection

Humor has long been a feature of political discourse, but modern campaigns have increasingly embraced it as a central strategy. By leveraging satire and clever messaging, humor simplifies complex issues and fosters a sense of relatability.

Breaking Down Complexity

Humor condenses multifaceted political topics into digestible messages, helping audiences engage without feeling overwhelmed. For instance, campaign content highlighting economic challenges under Biden, paired with a witty reference to Trump's energy policies, captured voters' attention while conveying policy critiques effectively.

Illustration: Consider a meme juxtaposing two images—one of Trump speaking at an oil rig, the other of rising gas prices at the pump—captioned, "Which energy future do you prefer?" This humorous critique made the issue relatable and memorable.

Shaping Public Perception

Trump's team often used satirical content to frame opponents in ways that resonated with voters. For example, nicknames or slogans targeting specific political figures became shorthand for broader criticisms, embedding these ideas into public consciousness.

Example: Satirical online posts mocking broad policy promises with simplified, humorous visuals fostered engagement and shaped discussions about campaign priorities.

Emotional Appeals: Engaging Voter Sentiment

Emotion is a cornerstone of political persuasion, connecting candidates to voters on a deeper, more visceral level. In the 2024 election, Trump's campaign effectively balanced humor with emotional resonance to energize its base and draw in undecided voters.

Appealing to Nostalgia

Campaigns often invoke nostalgia to remind voters of "better times" and suggest a return to stability or progress. Trump's messaging frequently referenced economic growth and national pride during his presidency, contrasting these with perceived current challenges.

Example: Ads featuring workers sharing stories of economic success under Trump and hopeful imagery of American industry evoked a strong emotional response from audiences in swing states like Michigan.

Evoking Urgency and Concern

Emotional appeals also portrayed opponents' policies as immediate threats to voters' well-being or values. For example, targeting parental rights in education through localized campaigns amplified suburban voters' feelings of protection and concern.

Case Study: Targeted ads were shown to suburban mothers, emphasizing Trump's role in preserving educational autonomy while contrasting it with the perceived risks posed by Harris's policies.

Humor as a Catalyst for Digital Engagement

In the digital age, humor has found a natural home on social media platforms, where witty content spreads rapidly and engages users across demographics.

Viral Potential of Humor

Humorous content generates high engagement on Twitter, Facebook, and TikTok. Campaigns capitalize on this by producing shareable content that travels organically.

Example: A short TikTok video parodying inflation rates using a popular dance trend achieved millions of views, drawing attention to economic concerns without relying on traditional ads.

Empowering Grassroots Participation

Humor also empowers supporters to create content, amplifying campaign messages through grassroots efforts. This user-generated content often enhances authenticity and relatability.

Illustration: Supporters inspired by campaign memes contributed their satirical posts, expanding the reach and impact of Trump's messaging.

Risks and Critiques of Simplification

While humor and emotion are powerful, they have drawbacks. Critics argue that reducing complex issues to soundbites risks undermining substantive policy debates.

The Danger of Oversimplification

Humor's tendency to focus on surface-level critiques can sometimes trivialize serious issues, leaving voters with an incomplete understanding of the stakes.

Critique: Analysts have noted that while humorous memes drive engagement, they often fail to encourage deeper policy discussions among voters.

Potential for Polarization

Emotional appeals, when framed divisively, can deepen existing partisan divides. Campaigns must balance effective messaging with the responsibility to foster constructive dialogue.

Broader Implications for Political Campaigning

The strategic use of humor and emotion in the 2024 election underscores their lasting impact on modern political communication.

Lessons for Future Campaigns

Balance Relatability and Depth: Humor and emotion should serve as entry points for broader discussions, not replacements for substantive policy debates.

Leverage Digital Tools: Social media platforms provide unmatched opportunities for engagement. Campaigns that adapt to these trends can effectively amplify their reach.

Foster Ethical Communication: Campaigns must ensure their messaging inspires connection rather than deepening divisions.

The Way Forward

The 2024 election highlighted the importance of meeting voters where they are, using humor and emotion to bridge gaps in understanding and engagement. By blending creativity with responsibility, future campaigns can elevate political discourse while harnessing these tools to drive voter participation.

Digital Strategy Optimization Model (DSOM)

A Blueprint for Modern Campaigning

The **Digital Strategy Optimization Model (DSOM)**, a dynamic, three-stage framework that revolutionized campaign approaches to voter engagement, was at the heart of Trump's 2024 digital success.

The Three Stages of DSOM

Identification of Target Audiences

The campaign segmented the electorate into specific groups based on demographics, interests, and behaviors using advanced data analytics. This segmentation enabled highly targeted outreach.

Young Professionals: Highlighted issues like student loan reform and affordable housing.

Parents: Focused on education reform and parental rights.

Retirees: Emphasized healthcare and social security stability.

Crafting Tailored Content

Each segment received personalized messages designed to address their unique concerns. Ads were localized, with specific policy promises tied to regional or demographic needs.

Example: Voters in the Rust Belt were shown ads emphasizing job creation and manufacturing, while suburban voters received content about school safety and family support.

Evaluation of Engagement Outcomes

The campaign continuously monitored real-time engagement metrics to refine its strategy. Ads that performed poorly were adjusted or replaced and resonated messages were amplified. This iterative process ensured that resources were allocated effectively.

Implications for Future Campaigns

DSOM provides a roadmap for future campaigns, demonstrating the importance of adaptability, data-driven precision, and continuous optimization. As digital platforms evolve, campaigns must embrace this dynamic approach to remain competitive.

The Double-Edged Sword of Digital Campaigning

While digital platforms offer unprecedented opportunities for engagement, they also present significant risks, including polarization, misinformation, and ethical concerns.

Polarization and Echo Chambers

Algorithms designed to maximize engagement often funnel users into echo chambers, reinforcing their existing beliefs. This dynamic exacerbates political polarization, making it harder for campaigns to foster dialogue across divides.

Example:

A 2024 study by the Pew Research Center found that 62% of Americans consumed news primarily through social media, with 45% rarely encountering opposing viewpoints. This insular environment allowed narratives to flourish unchecked, deepening divisions within the electorate.

Misinformation in the Digital Age: A Double-Edged Sword

Digital platforms have revolutionized how campaigns engage voters, enabling unprecedented reach and precision. However, this transformation comes with significant risks, particularly the proliferation of misinformation and manipulation. Viral content—often designed to evoke strong emotional reactions—has become a staple of modern political strategy. Yet, while such content can effectively mobilize support, it frequently blurs the line between truth and fiction.

How do digital campaigns balance the need for engagement with ethical responsibility? What are the long-term implications of misinformation on voter trust and democratic integrity? This analysis delves into the mechanisms by which misinformation spreads, the moral dilemmas it presents, and the strategies needed to mitigate its impact while preserving free expression.

How Digital Platforms Facilitate Misinformation

The architecture of digital platforms prioritizes engagement, inadvertently amplifying sensational or misleading content. Algorithms favor posts with high shares, likes, and comments, creating an ecosystem where misinformation thrives.

Algorithmic Bias

Social media algorithms reward emotionally charged content, often including misinformation, because it drives user activity.

Example: During the 2024 election, posts falsely claiming widespread voter fraud gained traction on Twitter and Facebook, generating millions of interactions despite being debunked by credible sources.

Echo Chambers and Confirmation Bias

Platforms often create echo chambers by showing users content aligning with their beliefs. This reinforces biases and limits exposure to opposing perspectives.

Case Study: A Pew Research study found that 45% of Americans received news exclusively from social media in 2024, with many engaging only with content aligned with their political leaning. While critics argue that platforms should take a stronger stance against misinformation, others caution against overreaching and emphasize the importance of preserving free speech. Balancing content moderation with open dialogue remains a contentious challenge.

Viral Content and Its Ethical Implications
Viral content is a powerful tool in modern campaigns, but its use often raises ethical questions, particularly when it skirts the boundaries of truth.

Emotional Manipulation
Misinformation often exploits fear, anger, or hope to elicit strong emotional responses. These emotions can override critical thinking, making users more likely to share content without verifying its accuracy.

Example: A viral meme falsely suggesting that Kamala Harris planned to eliminate private healthcare spread rapidly on Facebook, sparking heated debates despite being factually incorrect.

Discrediting Opponents
Campaigns sometimes use misinformation strategically to discredit opponents, knowing that even refuted claims can leave lasting impressions.

Historical Comparison: The "Swift Boat Veterans for Truth" campaign against John Kerry in 2004 leveraged misleading claims that significantly impacted public perception despite later being debunked.

Long-Term Trust Erosion

The widespread use of misinformation undermines trust in political institutions, media, and democracy. This erosion of trust can discourage voter participation and exacerbate polarization.

Real-World Impact of Misinformation in 2024

The 2024 election offered numerous examples of how misinformation influenced voter behavior and shaped the political narrative.

Example: The Hunter Biden Laptop Scandal

When allegations surrounding Hunter Biden's laptop resurfaced during the campaign, they quickly spread across social media platforms. While some claims were substantiated, others were exaggerated or fabricated, creating confusion among voters.

Impact: This narrative dominated news cycles for weeks, forcing Biden's campaign to divert resources to damage control, even as Trump's base galvanized around the issue.

Example: Misleading Polls and Election Predictions

Viral posts claiming that Trump's campaign was doomed by early polling created a false sense of security among Harris supporters, potentially impacting voter turnout.

Statistical Insight: A report by the Brookings Institution found that misinformation about polling results reduced voter confidence in battleground states.

Addressing the spread of misinformation requires a multi-faceted approach involving campaigns, digital platforms, and voters.

Transparency in Campaign Messaging
Campaigns must prioritize accuracy in their messaging and provide verifiable data to support claims. Transparency fosters trust and counters the perception that all political communication is manipulative.

Example: During the 2024 election, some campaigns adopted fact-checking partnerships to ensure their content met journalistic standards.

Platform Accountability
While social media companies play a crucial role in addressing misinformation, implementing stronger algorithms to detect and flag false content presents challenges. Concerns about censorship, algorithmic transparency, and unintended bias must be addressed to ensure these measures balance moderation with open discourse.

Media Literacy Education
Empowering voters to evaluate content critically can mitigate the impact of misinformation. Programs that teach media literacy in schools and communities are essential for fostering informed citizenry.

Efforts to promote media literacy, such as school and community workshops, have shown promise in combating misinformation.

Evaluations of similar programs have highlighted improvements in participants' ability to identify misleading claims, underscoring the importance of education in mitigating digital disinformation.

Implications for Democracy
The unchecked spread of misinformation threatens not only electoral outcomes but also the foundations of democratic governance.

Impact on Voter Trust
When misinformation dominates the narrative, voters lose confidence in the integrity of elections and democratic institutions. Restoring this trust requires collective action from all stakeholders.

Global Comparisons
The challenges posed by misinformation are not unique to the United States. Nations like Brazil and the Philippines have grappled with similar issues, highlighting the need for international collaboration to address this global problem.

The Role of Free Expression
Balancing the need to combat misinformation by preserving free speech is a critical dilemma. Developing nuanced content moderation policies that respect this balance will be key to sustaining democratic values.

Lessons for the Digital Age
Misinformation and manipulation are defining challenges of modern political campaigns, amplified by the reach and speed of digital

platforms. While the 2024 election showcased the potential of viral content to engage and mobilize, it highlighted the ethical dilemmas and risks associated with these strategies.

To safeguard democracy, campaigns must prioritize truth and transparency, digital platforms enforce stricter content moderation, and voters must develop the skills to navigate an increasingly complex information landscape. Only through a concerted, collective effort can we mitigate the harms of misinformation and ensure a healthier, more informed democratic process.

Ethical Considerations in Micro-Targeting

Data Privacy and Transparency Campaigns
Modern political campaigns are no longer one-size-fits-all endeavors. Thanks to data analytics and advanced algorithms, campaigns can target voters with unparalleled precision, tailoring messages to individual preferences, demographics, and behavioral patterns. While this capability has revolutionized voter engagement, it raises profound ethical questions.

How much should voters know about how their data is being used? At what point does persuasion become manipulation? These questions cut to the core of democracy, highlighting the tension between innovation and integrity in political communication. This section explores the ethical dilemmas of micro-targeting, weighing the benefits of tailored outreach against the risks to privacy, transparency, and democratic trust.

Micro-Targeting: A Powerful but Controversial Tool

Micro-targeting allows campaigns to deliver specific messages to narrowly defined voter segments, increasing the likelihood of resonance and engagement. While effective, this approach also intensifies concerns about privacy and manipulation.

How Micro-Targeting Works

Campaigns gather vast data from social media, public records, and online behaviors to segment voters into distinct categories. This information is then used to craft messages that appeal to specific concerns or preferences.

Example: In the 2024 election, Trump's campaign targeted rural voters with ads emphasizing agricultural subsidies, while suburban parents received content focused on education policy.

Advantages

Micro-targeting enhances efficiency, allowing campaigns to allocate resources strategically. It also helps engage underrepresented groups by addressing their unique concerns.

Case Study: During the 2016 Brexit campaign, micro-targeting was credited with mobilizing voters in regions that traditional campaigns had overlooked.

Criticism: Data Collection and Consent

Critics argue that voters often do not know how much their data is being used. Platforms like Facebook, which played a central role in the 2016 Cambridge Analytica scandal, have faced backlash for allowing third parties to access personal information without explicit user consent.

Statistical Insight: A 2020 Pew Research survey found that 79% of Americans were concerned about how companies and campaigns use their data, underscoring the public's unease with opaque practices.

The issue of privacy is at the heart of the debate. Voter data, including email addresses and browsing history, is collected and used in ways many individuals do not fully understand.

Lack of Informed Consent

Most voters are unaware of how their information is collected, stored, or used. Terms of service agreements, often buried in legal jargon, fail to provide meaningful transparency.

Example: In 2024, it was revealed that several campaigns had partnered with data brokers to access geolocation data, raising questions about whether voters had consented to such tracking.

Potential for Abuse

The more granular the data, the greater the potential for manipulation. For instance, targeting individuals based on psychological vulnerabilities—such as anxiety or fear—pushes ethical boundaries.

Case Study: A 2018 analysis of Facebook ads during the 2016 election showed that emotionally charged content designed to provoke fear or anger performed better than neutral messaging, raising concerns about psychological manipulation.

Transparency is a critical component of ethical micro-targeting but is also one of the most contentious.

Should Campaigns Disclose Their Methods?

Disclosing how voter data is collected and used would promote accountability but could also hinder campaign strategies. Campaigns argue that revealing targeting methods may give opponents an advantage.

Counterpoint: Transparency would empower voters to make informed decisions about the content they engage with, fostering trust in the democratic process.

Global Comparisons: GDPR and Beyond

The European Union's General Data Protection Regulation (GDPR) provides a framework for data privacy. It requires organizations to disclose how personal data is processed and offers individuals the right to opt-out. While not specific to campaigns, GDPR represents a model for balancing innovation with transparency.

Example: In the UK, campaigns must now declare whether political organizations fund digital ads, a step toward greater accountability.

Persuasion vs. Manipulation: A Blurred Line

One of the most difficult ethical questions surrounding micro-targeting is determining where persuasion ends and manipulation begins.

The Role of Emotional Appeals
Emotional appeals are a staple of political campaigning, but micro-targeting amplifies their impact by tailoring messages to individual fears or aspirations. While persuasive, this approach risks crossing into manipulation when it exploits vulnerabilities.

Example: Ads targeting senior citizens with exaggerated claims about healthcare cuts during the 2024 election illustrate how emotional manipulation can distort voter perceptions.

Balancing Effectiveness and Ethics
Campaigns must balance effectiveness and ethical standards. Clear guidelines are needed to ensure that micro-targeting remains a tool for persuasion rather than coercion.

Proposed Solution: Independent oversight bodies could audit campaign practices, ensuring compliance with ethical norms.

Broader Implications for Democracy
The ethical considerations of micro-targeting have far-reaching implications for the health of democratic systems.

Erosion of Trust

When voters feel manipulated or misled, trust in the electoral process erodes. Restoring this trust requires greater transparency and accountability from both campaigns and platforms.

Polarization and Echo Chambers

Micro-targeting, which tailors messages to specific demographics, can contribute to polarization by reinforcing existing biases. Efforts to address this must include promoting cross-cutting content that bridges ideological divides.

Policy Recommendations

Mandatory Transparency: Require campaigns to disclose how voter data is collected and used.

Stronger Privacy Protections: Implement regulations similar to GDPR to ensure voters have control over their personal information.

Ethical Oversight: Establish independent bodies to monitor campaign practices and enforce ethical guidelines.

Navigating the Ethical Tightrope

Micro-targeting is a powerful tool that has transformed political campaigns, but its ethical implications cannot be ignored. Balancing innovation with integrity requires explicit guidelines, robust oversight, and a commitment to transparency from all stakeholders.

As campaigns evolve in the digital age, the challenge will be to harness the benefits of micro-targeting while safeguarding voter trust and democratic principles. By prioritizing ethical practices, campaigns can ensure that their strategies enhance, rather than undermine, the integrity of elections.

Shaping Narratives and Influencing Perceptions

Real-Time Adaptation in Digital Campaigning
Political campaigns must adapt rapidly to maintain relevance in an era dominated by instant communication and constantly evolving news cycles. The 2024 presidential election illustrated how real-time adaptation can shape narratives, influence perceptions, and sway voter behavior. Donald Trump's campaign demonstrated an unparalleled ability to monitor online trends, respond to emerging issues, and pivot messaging in real-time.

What sets a successful digital campaign apart? It is not merely the ability to disseminate information but the capacity to respond dynamically to the electorate's pulse. This section examines the mechanics of real-time adaptation, exploring how the Trump campaign leveraged digital tools to stay ahead of the narrative curve while highlighting broader implications for political strategy and democratic engagement.

Leveraging Digital Tools for Real-Time Feedback
Gathering and analyzing data rapidly is the backbone of real-time adaptation. Digital platforms like Twitter, Facebook, and Instagram offer campaigns an unparalleled window into voter sentiment.

Social Media Monitoring and Analytics

Using advanced analytics tools, campaigns can track trending topics, hashtags, and public sentiment. These platforms provide immediate feedback on how messages resonate with target audiences.

Example: During the 2024 campaign, Trump's team identified a surge in online discussions about inflation and rising energy costs. Within hours, they released targeted ads emphasizing Trump's economic policies, aligning their messaging with voters' immediate concerns.

Harnessing User-Generated Content

Real-time feedback also allows campaigns to amplify user-generated content (UGC). When voters share memes, videos, or tweets supporting a campaign, these organic messages often carry greater authenticity than paid advertisements.

Case Study: A viral TikTok video by a Michigan farmer praising Trump's agricultural subsidies gained millions of views. The campaign quickly integrated this content into its broader messaging strategy, showcasing grassroots support.

The Risk of Overreaction

While real-time adaptation is valuable, critics caution that an overreliance on immediate trends may lead campaigns to prioritize short-term gains over long-term strategy. Maintaining a balance between agility and consistency is crucial.

Shaping Narratives Through Rapid Response

Real-time adaptation enables campaigns to seize control of narratives before opponents can react, a strategy that proved decisive in the 2024 election.

Proactive Messaging

By monitoring online trends, campaigns can preemptively address issues, framing debates in their favor.

Example: When Kamala Harris's controversial policy proposal sparked online criticism, Trump's campaign immediately released statements emphasizing their contrasting policies, effectively redirecting the narrative.

Capitalizing on Opponent Missteps

Real-time monitoring allows campaigns to exploit opponents' gaffes or vulnerabilities swiftly.

Case Study: Following a Harris debate misstep where she struggled to articulate her position on energy independence, Trump's campaign flooded social media with clips highlighting the moment, reinforcing their narrative of Trump's leadership in energy policy.

Crisis Management

Adaptation is equally critical during crises. Effective campaigns address adverse developments promptly, preventing narratives from spiraling out of control.

Historical Comparison: During the 2016 election, Hillary Clinton's delayed response to email controversies contributed to a perception of secrecy. Trump's 2024 team learned from these examples and responded swiftly to challenges like media scrutiny over policy details.

Real-Time Adaptation and Voter Engagement
Beyond shaping narratives, real-time adaptation enhances voter engagement by creating a sense of immediacy and relevance.

Interactive Campaigning
Modern digital platforms facilitate dialogue between campaigns and voters, offering features like Q&A sessions, live streams, and interactive polls. These tools enhance engagement and provide campaigns with real-time insights into voter priorities.

Example: During a Facebook Live event, Trump addressed voter questions about rising gas prices, presenting solutions that felt timely and personalized.

Localized Messaging
Campaigns can tailor messages to specific regions or demographics based on real-time data.

Case Study: In Ohio, an increase in online discussions about opioid addiction prompted Trump's team to release ads focused on healthcare and rehabilitation programs, resonating deeply with affected communities.

The Echo Chamber Effect

Critics argue that digital adaptation risks reinforcing echo chambers, where campaigns target only those likely to agree with their message. This can deepen polarization by excluding opposing viewpoints. However, advocates contend that such precision ensures resource efficiency and maximizes impact.

Challenges and Ethical Considerations
While real-time adaptation offers clear advantages, it raises ethical questions and logistical challenges.

Misinformation Risks
Rapid response strategies may inadvertently amplify misinformation if campaigns act on unverified trends.

Example: During the 2024 election, a fake news story about Harris's stance on Medicare gained traction online. While Trump's campaign distanced itself from the narrative, its delayed response highlighted the dangers of acting without verification.

Privacy Concerns
Real-time data collection often relies on tracking user behavior, raising concerns about voter privacy.

Counterpoint: Advocates argue that anonymized data mitigates these risks, but stricter regulations on data use may be necessary to maintain public trust.

Over adaptation
Constantly shifting strategies to align with real-time trends may lead to inconsistencies, undermining a campaign's overall message. Therefore, developing a clear vision that adapts without losing coherence is essential.

Broader Implications for Campaign Strategy
The success of real-time adaptation in 2024 signals a paradigm shift in political campaigning.

Lessons for Future Campaigns
Integrate Data Analytics: Effective campaigns must invest in tools that provide actionable insights into voter behavior and sentiment.

Balance Agility with Vision: Adaptation should enhance, not replace, a campaign's core narrative.

Prioritize Transparency: To build trust, campaigns must be transparent about collecting and using real-time data.

Global Comparisons

Real-time adaptation is not unique to the U.S. In 2022, Emmanuel Macron's reelection campaign in France used similar strategies, tailoring messages to specific regions based on real-time polling and social media feedback.

Impact on Democracy

While real-time adaptation enhances engagement, it raises questions about fairness and accountability. Ensuring campaigns use these tools responsibly will be critical to preserving democratic integrity.

The Future of Real-Time Campaigning

The 2024 election demonstrated the transformative power of real-time adaptation, reshaping how campaigns connect with voters and respond to challenges. By harnessing digital tools and data analytics, campaigns can shape narratives that feel immediate and relevant, fostering deeper voter engagement.

However, with great power comes great responsibility. As real-time strategies become the norm, campaigns must prioritize ethical considerations, transparency, and long-term vision to strengthen their methods rather than undermine democracy. The challenge for future campaigns will be to strike this delicate balance, leveraging innovation to serve their candidates and the electorate.

The Path Forward: Embracing Digital Evolution

As campaigns continue to embrace digital platforms, they must navigate the challenges and opportunities of this new era. Key considerations include:

Data Ethics: Ensuring that voter data is used responsibly and transparently.

Engaging Across Divides: Leveraging digital platforms to foster dialogue rather than deepen divisions.

Combating Misinformation: Developing strategies to counteract false narratives while maintaining free expression.

New Campaigning Era: 2024 Lessons Playbook
The 2024 presidential election marked a watershed moment in political campaigning. With Donald Trump's reelection bid exemplifying digital strategy at its peak, his campaign set new benchmarks for leveraging technology to engage, persuade, and mobilize voters. The transformation wasn't merely about using digital platforms—it was about reshaping the fundamentals of political communication, creating a model that blends precision, immediacy, and adaptability.

What does this evolution mean for the future of political engagement? The game's rules are shifting as campaigns increasingly rely on data analytics, real-time adaptation, and micro-targeting. This section explores the strategies that defined the Trump campaign's digital dominance, the challenges they present, and the implications for future elections worldwide.

The Pillars of Trump's Digital Strategy in 2024
Donald Trump's 2024 campaign exemplified how digital tools can be used to amplify messages and tailor them to specific audiences with surgical precision.

How Trump Played the Media...Again

Targeted Messaging at Scale

The campaign identified key voter demographics by leveraging advanced data analytics and crafted messages tailored to their unique concerns.

Example: Rural voters received content emphasizing agricultural subsidies, while suburban parents saw ads about education and parental rights. This segmented approach ensured maximum resonance with diverse groups.

Real-Time Adaptation

The campaign's ability to pivot quickly in response to emerging trends or controversies was unparalleled. Monitoring voter sentiment on platforms like Twitter and Facebook allowed the team to refine messaging instantly.

Case Study: When inflation became a hot-button issue in the weeks leading up to the election, Trump's campaign immediately launched a series of ads addressing economic recovery plans.

Influencer Amplification

The Trump campaign tapped into networks of online influencers who acted as unofficial surrogates, organically spreading campaign messages to millions of followers.

Historical Comparison: This strategy echoed Obama's 2008 digital-first approach but took it to new heights by integrating grassroots influencers into the campaign's communication matrix.

Opportunities Offered by Digital Campaigning

The digital age offers campaigns a suite of tools that transform how they connect with voters, creating opportunities for deeper engagement and broader reach.

Unprecedented Reach

Digital platforms provide access to billions of users, enabling campaigns to reach voters in previously inaccessible regions.

Example: TikTok, once dismissed as a platform for younger audiences, became a key battleground in 2024, with viral campaign content reaching millions of first-time voters.

Cost-Effectiveness

Digital advertising offers a more cost-efficient way to disseminate messages than traditional media. With tools like pay-per-click ads, campaigns can ensure their budgets are spent reaching engaged users rather than passive audiences.

Interactive Engagement

Platforms like Instagram Live and YouTube Q&A sessions allow candidates and voters to interact directly, fostering a sense of accessibility and transparency.

Example: Trump's campaign hosted weekly live streams addressing voter questions, reinforcing his image as a leader attuned to public concerns.

Counterargument: Digital Divide

However, critics point out that not all voters have equal access to digital platforms, potentially marginalizing those in rural or underserved areas. Bridging this divide will be essential for ensuring equitable political engagement.

Challenges of Digital Campaigning

While digital strategies offer undeniable advantages, they also come with significant challenges that demand careful navigation.

Misinformation and Manipulation

Digital platforms are fertile ground for misinformation, distorting voter perceptions and undermining trust in democratic processes.

Case Study: During the 2024 election, viral memes misrepresenting Kamala Harris's policy positions spread widely, requiring her campaign to divert resources to damage control.

Ethical Concerns in Data Usage

Using voter data for micro-targeting raises privacy concerns and ethical questions about how much campaigns should know about individual voters.

Statistical Insight: A Pew Research survey in 2024 found that 78% of Americans were concerned about the lack of transparency in how campaigns used their data.

Echo Chambers and Polarization

Algorithms that prioritize content users are likely to engage with can create echo chambers, reinforcing biases and deepening societal divisions.

Regulatory Oversight

The rapid evolution of digital campaigning has outpaced regulatory frameworks, leaving gaps in oversight that could be exploited. As a result, calls for stricter regulations on political advertising and data usage are growing louder.

Global Implications of the Digital Shift

The strategies seen in the 2024 U.S. election are not confined to America—they are part of a global trend reshaping politics worldwide.

Case Study: Macron's Campaign in France

Emmanuel Macron's 2022 reelection campaign employed similar digital strategies, using data analytics to tailor messaging and engage voters across diverse demographics.

Lessons for Emerging Democracies

In countries with burgeoning democratic systems, digital platforms offer an opportunity to level the playing field, enabling grassroots movements to challenge entrenched political elites. However, the risks of misinformation and manipulation are even more pronounced in these contexts.

Global Challenges
The international community must grapple with questions of sovereignty, as foreign actors have increasingly used digital platforms to influence elections. Combating this requires global cooperation and robust cybersecurity measures.

Looking Forward: The Future of Digital Campaigning
The lessons of the 2024 election highlight the need for campaigns to embrace digital strategies while addressing their ethical and practical challenges.

Investing in Media Literacy
Educating voters to evaluate digital content critically is essential for countering misinformation and fostering informed decision-making.

Balancing Innovation with Integrity
Campaigns must innovate without sacrificing transparency or ethical responsibility. Building trust with voters will be critical to the success of future strategies.

Regulatory Reform
Governments and organizations should develop frameworks to ensure accountability in digital campaigning, from transparency in data usage to oversight of political ads.

A Blueprint for the Digital Age
The 2024 election marked the dawn of a new era in political campaigning, where digital platforms are no longer just tools—they

are the battleground. By mastering the art of real-time adaptation, targeted messaging, and interactive engagement, the Trump campaign set a new standard for political communication.

However, this new frontier also demands greater accountability, transparency, and ethical consideration. The future of campaigning lies in striking a delicate balance between innovation and integrity, ensuring that digital strategies serve the electorate rather than manipulate it. As we move forward, the challenge will be to refine these tools and to wield them responsibly, preserving the democratic principles at the heart of every election.

Chapter 2 References

"How Trump's Campaign Used Social Media to Win Again" – Wired https://www.wired.com/story/donald-trump-online-campaign-era

"How disinformation defined the 2024 election narrative" – Brookings Institution https://www.brookings.edu/articles/how-disinformation-defined-the-2024-election-narrative/

"Your data is political: W&M computer scientists find gaps in the privacy practices of campaign websites" – William & Mary News https://news.wm.edu/2024/02/07/your-personal-data-is-political-wm-computer-scientists-find-gaps-in-the-privacy-practices-of-campaign-websites/

"Media Influence on Politics: 7 Election Trends in 2024" – University of Oregon School of Journalism and Communication https://journalism.uoregon.edu/news/media-influence-on-politics

"How Political Campaigns Use Your Data to Target You" – Electronic Frontier Foundation https://www.eff.org/deeplinks/2024/04/how-political-campaigns-use-your-data-target-you

"The Evolving Role of Social Media in the 2024 U.S. Elections" – Policy Center for the New South https://www.policycenter.ma/podcasts/evolving-role-social-media-2024-us-elections

"Protecting Voter Data Privacy in the Age of AI" – Corporate Compliance Insights https://www.corporatecomplianceinsights.com/protecting-voter-data-privacy-in-the-age-of-ai/

"Social media disinformation looms over presidential election" – University of Michigan News https://news.umich.edu/social-media-disinformation-looms-over-presidential-election/

"Voter data privacy concerns over apps used by political parties" – Open Rights Group https://www.openrightsgroup.org/press-releases/new-report-voter-data-privacy-concerns-over-apps-used-by-political-parties/

"The 2024 Election and the Changing Definition of 'The Media'" – PR News https://www.prnewsonline.com/the-2024-election-and-the-changing-definition-of-the-media/

Donald Trump's Incorrigible Presidency: Examining the Impact and Controversies, Frank Visser / ChatGPT. https://integralworld.net/visser254.html

America's fantasy hero. https://www.lowyinstitute.org/the-interpreter/america-s-fantasy-hero

Calzada, I., & Almirall, E. (2020). Europe needs a revolution in the administration.

Chapter 3: The Power of the Pocketbook

Economic Messaging in the 2024 Election

Winning Voters' Pocketbooks
Economic messaging has always been a defining factor in presidential elections, cutting across demographics, ideologies, and geographic divides. The 2024 election was no exception. It vividly reminded voters that they prioritize candidates who speak to their immediate financial realities when faced with economic uncertainty. Donald Trump's campaign capitalized on this principle, presenting a narrative of economic revival that resonated deeply with diverse voter groups.

By contrast, while rooted in progressive ideals and long-term systemic reforms, Kamala Harris's campaign struggled to connect with voters' immediate economic anxieties. This juxtaposition of strategies offers a window into the dynamics of modern campaigns, where the ability to address both short-term concerns and long-term aspirations can mean the difference between victory and defeat.

This section explores how economic messaging shaped the 2024 election, highlighting Trump's strategic focus on voter priorities, the emotional and practical dimensions of economic promises, and the broader implications for future campaigns.

Economic Messaging: A Lifeline in Times of Crisis
Economic issues can uniquely unify and mobilize voters, particularly during periods of financial strain. In 2024, inflation, wage stagnation,

and post-pandemic economic recovery were at the forefront of voter concerns.

Which economic strategy resonates more with voters?

Trump's Immediate Relief
Focus on short-term financial stability and job creation

Harris's Long-term Reforms
Emphasize systemic change and equity

Why Economic Messaging Resonates

Economic promises tap into emotional and practical concerns, addressing voters' fears about survival while offering hope for prosperity. For many, these messages are not just policy proposals—they are lifelines.

Example: Trump's campaign emphasized tangible benefits like job creation, tax cuts, and trade protections. This contrasted sharply with Harris's focus on climate policies, which, while forward-thinking, failed to address voters' immediate economic struggles.

The Storm Analogy

Imagine a storm threatening a community. While some leaders might discuss long-term climate strategies, the most effective response would focus on immediate relief: shelter, food, and safety. Similarly, voters prioritize short-term solutions over ideological aspirations in times of economic uncertainty.

Historical Context

This dynamic has played out in past elections as well. During the 1992 presidential race, Bill Clinton's famous slogan, "It's the economy, stupid," underscored the centrality of economic issues in winning over voters. Trump's campaign in 2024 echoed this sentiment, tailoring its messaging to address voters' immediate concerns.

Trump's Strategic Focus on Economic Priorities

Trump's campaign leveraged advanced data analytics to identify voter groups, tailoring messages to address their economic concerns. For example, in Michigan's Rust Belt, Trump's messaging highlighted trade protections and the revival of domestic manufacturing jobs, which resonated with workers in an industry that had seen decades of decline. Meanwhile, Harris's campaign promoted clean energy jobs as a forward-looking solution, but critics argued that this messaging failed to address immediate economic insecurities in traditional manufacturing communities. Exit polls from Michigan showed that 62% of voters who identified economic concerns as their top priority favored Trump, highlighting the importance of connecting with voter anxieties.

Localized Messaging for Maximum Impact

Rather than relying on generic economic slogans, Trump's team tailored its messaging to specific regions and demographics.

Example: In Rust Belt states like Pennsylvania and Ohio, ads emphasized job creation in manufacturing and trade protections. In agricultural regions like Wisconsin, the campaign focused on subsidies and tariffs that protected farmers' livelihoods.

Emotional Engagement with Disillusioned Voters

Trump's rhetoric frequently acknowledged the economic pain experienced by working-class Americans. By validating their struggles and promising revival, he built trust and loyalty.

In Michigan, Trump's campaign featured testimonials from workers who attributed their employment to his economic policies. These personal stories brought his broader economic message to life, emphasizing the tangible benefits of his trade and industry initiatives.

Risks of Overpromising

Critics argue that while effective in mobilizing voters, Trump's bold economic promises often lacked detailed implementation plans. However, the campaign's ability to frame these promises as achievable goals resonated strongly with voters seeking hope amidst uncertainty.

The Emotional and Practical Dimensions of Economic Messaging

Economic promises serve dual functions: they offer practical solutions while appealing to voters' emotions.

Practical Anchors

Voters evaluate candidates based on the feasibility and relevance of their economic proposals. Trump's focus on specific policies, such as tax cuts and infrastructure investments, gave voters tangible solutions to their concerns.

Emotional Anchors

Beyond practicality, economic messaging taps into broader pride, stability, and identity themes.

Example: Trump framed economic revival as a matter of national pride, evoking nostalgia for America's industrial heyday. This messaging resonated particularly with Rust Belt voters, who saw their livelihoods as symbols of American strength.

Contrast with Harris's Messaging

While Harris's emphasis on green energy initiatives aimed to address long-term climate goals, it faced resistance in fossil-fuel-dependent states like Pennsylvania, where coal and natural gas are vital to local economies. However, it's important to note that younger voters in these areas supported her policies, seeing renewable energy as a pathway to job creation. According to a report by NPR, 43% of Pennsylvania voters aged 18-29 cited clean energy jobs as a key motivator for supporting Harris. This divide between generational priorities underscores the challenges of balancing immediate economic concerns with future-focused policies.

Lessons for Future Campaigns

The 2024 election offers valuable insights into the role of economic messaging in modern campaigns.

Aligning Messaging with Voter Realities

Effective economic messaging must address both immediate concerns and long-term aspirations. Campaigns focusing solely on abstract policies risk alienating voters, prioritizing tangible benefits.

Building Credibility Through Tangible Benefits

Voters are more likely to trust candidates whose promises are backed by actionable plans.

Example: Trump's emphasis on trade negotiations and job creation provided voters with clear, measurable goals.

Leveraging Digital Platforms for Economic Messaging

Digital tools allow campaigns to amplify their messages with unprecedented precision. Using data analytics to identify voter concerns, campaigns can craft messages that resonate deeply with specific demographics.

Historical Comparison

The success of economic messaging in 2024 mirrors similar trends in past elections, from Franklin D. Roosevelt's New Deal rhetoric during the Great Depression to Barack Obama's focus on middle-class recovery in 2008.

Broader Implications for Democracy

The centrality of economic messaging has far-reaching implications for democratic engagement and governance.

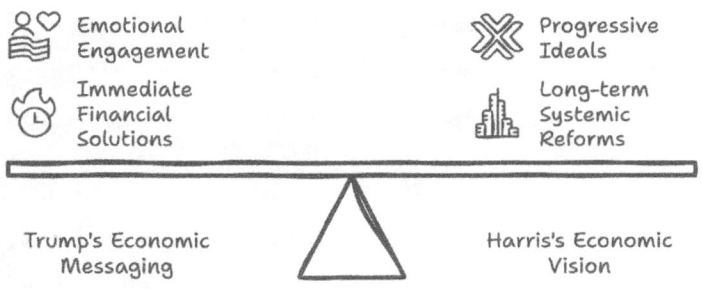

Comparing Economic Strategies in 2024 Election

Strengthening Voter Trust

When campaigns authentically address voters' economic concerns, they build trust in the democratic process.

The Danger of Oversimplification

While economic promises are powerful, oversimplifying complex issues risks undermining public understanding. Future campaigns must balance accessibility and nuance.

Shaping the Policy Agenda

Economic messaging not only wins elections but also shapes the policy priorities of incoming administrations. The themes emphasized during campaigns often set the tone for governance, influencing trade, taxation, and labor policy debates.

A Blueprint for Future Campaigns

The 2024 election reaffirmed the enduring power of economic messaging in presidential campaigns. Donald Trump demonstrated how economic narratives can mobilize, inspire, and unite by aligning his promises with voter realities and amplifying his message through digital platforms.

The lessons for future campaigns are clear: Address immediate concerns while offering a vision for long-term prosperity, build credibility through tangible benefits, and leverage digital tools to connect with voters authentically. By doing so, candidates can win elections and foster trust, engagement, and hope in the democratic process.

Economic Messaging: A Political Force That Resonates

Economic issues have long been pivotal in presidential elections, but in 2024, they took on heightened significance. After years of pandemic-related uncertainty, rising inflation, and an uneven recovery, voters were more attuned than ever to promises of financial stability and growth.

Economic promises serve dual purposes:

Emotional Function: They tap into voters' hopes for a better future, offering a vision of security and prosperity.

Practical Function: They address voters' immediate concerns, such as job security, wages, and affordability.

The Storm Analogy

Imagine a storm threatening a town. Some leaders might discuss long-term climate strategies to prevent future storms, but the most effective response would focus on immediate needs: shelter, food, and safety. Economic messaging works similarly. During financial hardship, voters prioritize survival and stability over ideological aspirations.

In 2024, this principle was evident as Trump's campaign emphasized immediate economic solutions, while Harris's broader, future-oriented messaging struggled to gain traction in key regions.

Turning Economic Challenges into Campaign Opportunities

Economic issues have long been the cornerstone of American presidential campaigns, but the 2024 election took this principle to new heights. As the U.S. grappled with post-pandemic recovery, inflation, and stagnating wages, economic anxieties became the defining concern for millions of voters. Donald Trump's campaign, understanding this landscape, deployed a finely tuned strategy to address the distinct economic worries of different voter groups. His success lay not in broad slogans but in highly localized and targeted messaging that felt deeply personal to those who heard it.

What made Trump's approach stand out? His campaign's ability to transform abstract policies into tangible promises resonated with voters' lived experiences. This section explores how Trump's team mapped economic anxieties across demographics and regions, using hyper-localized messaging to build trust and loyalty among key voter groups.

Understanding the Landscape of Economic Anxieties
To craft an effective campaign strategy, Trump's team first sought to understand the electorate's varied economic concerns. Unlike one-size-fits-all approaches, this required granular insights into regional and demographic priorities.

The Rust Belt: A Case Study in Manufacturing Revival
Historically reliant on manufacturing, the Rust Belt states have faced decades of industrial decline. Trump's campaign capitalized on this economic pain by emphasizing his administration's trade renegotiations and promises to revitalize domestic industries.

Example: In Michigan, ads celebrated Trump's tariffs on Chinese steel imports, claiming they protected American jobs. Town hall events featured testimonials from workers who credited Trump's policies with saving their livelihoods.

Agricultural Communities and Trade Concerns
In states like Iowa and Wisconsin, where farming is a way of life, Trump focused on tariffs and subsidies. While his trade wars initially caused anxiety among farmers, the campaign reframed these policies as part of a larger strategy to secure long-term stability for American agriculture.

Case Study: Trump's 2024 rallies in Wisconsin featured local dairy farmers who praised his administration for subsidies that helped offset international competition.

Short-Term Gains vs. Long-Term Impact

Critics argue that Trump's economic policies often prioritized short-term political wins over sustainable solutions. For example, while tariffs may have temporarily relieved some industries, they also increased costs for consumers and businesses reliant on imports. However, Trump's ability to frame these policies as patriotic efforts to "put America first" resonated with voters seeking immediate solutions.

The Emotional Resonance of Localized Messaging

Trump's campaign understood that economic messaging is not just about policies—it's about connecting with voters emotionally.

Acknowledging Struggles to Build Trust

Trump's rhetoric explicitly acknowledged voters' economic hardships, validating their experiences and frustrations. This approach was efficient among working-class voters who felt abandoned by previous administrations.

Example: During a rally in Pennsylvania, Trump declared, "I see you, I hear you, and I'm fighting for you," addressing steelworkers directly and promising to bring back manufacturing jobs.

Framing Policies as Moral Imperatives
Economic policies were often framed as pragmatic solutions and moral obligations to protect American workers and industries.

Historical Comparison: This mirrors Franklin D. Roosevelt's New Deal rhetoric, which also framed economic recovery as a moral duty to uplift the nation.

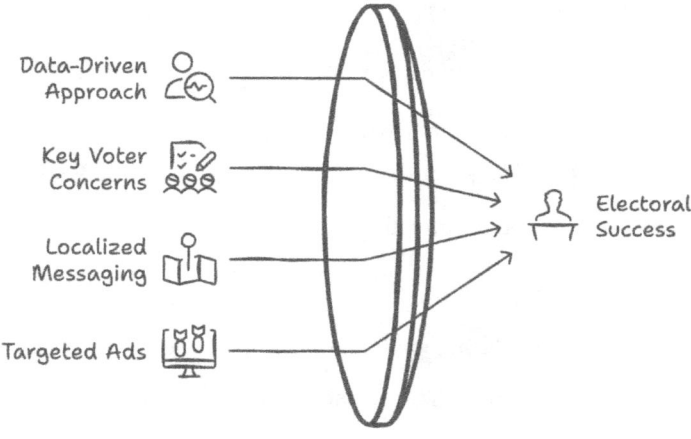

The Role of Rhetoric vs. Results
While Trump's rhetoric was undeniably effective, critics argue that it sometimes outpaced the tangible results of his policies. For instance, while manufacturing jobs grew during his presidency, the growth rate fell short of his ambitious promises. However, the emotional

resonance of his messaging often overshadowed these gaps in perception.

Hyper-Localized Messaging in Action

One of the defining features of Trump's 2024 campaign was its ability to tailor messages to the unique economic concerns of specific regions and demographics.

Rust Belt States: Manufacturing and Pride

In Rust Belt states like Ohio and Pennsylvania, Trump's campaign ran ads featuring workers in hard hats, emphasizing the dignity of labor and the importance of domestic production.

Example: A viral ad showcased a former auto worker from Michigan who claimed Trump's policies had saved his job, creating a narrative of hope and resilience.

Agricultural Communities: Securing the Heartland

The campaign focused on subsidies and trade protections in agricultural regions. Farmers were not just voters; they became symbols of America's backbone.

Case Study: A Facebook ad targeting Iowa farmers emphasized how Trump's trade negotiations with China included provisions for agricultural exports, presenting him as a champion of rural America.

Suburban Voters: Education and Stability

In suburban districts, Trump's campaign shifted focus to economic policies that appealed to families, such as tax credits and education reform. This strategy allowed the campaign to make inroads with suburban parents concerned about their children's futures.

Digital Precision

Using data analytics, the campaign identified micro-regions where specific economic concerns were most pronounced, allowing for highly targeted outreach.

Example: In Florida, digital ads addressing retirees focused on promises to protect Social Security and Medicare, directly appealing to older voters' financial anxieties.

Lessons for Future Campaigns

The success of Trump's 2024 campaign offers valuable lessons for future political strategists.

Granularity Over Generalization

Effective economic messaging requires understanding and addressing the specific needs of diverse voter groups. Generic slogans may inspire, but tailored messages build trust and loyalty.

Emotional Connection Matters

Policies alone are not enough. Voters respond to candidates who acknowledge their struggles and present solutions that resonate emotionally.

Balancing Short-Term and Long-Term Messaging

While addressing immediate concerns is critical, campaigns must also articulate a vision for long-term stability to build credibility.

How Trump Played the Media...Again

Leveraging Digital Platforms

Digital tools enable campaigns to identify and address voter concerns with unprecedented precision, making them indispensable in modern politics.

A Blueprint for Economic Messaging

Trump's strategic mapping of economic anxieties in the 2024 election demonstrated the power of targeted, localized messaging. By addressing the unique concerns of voters in the Rust Belt, agricultural regions, and suburban communities, his campaign forged deep connections that translated into electoral success.

For future campaigns, the lessons are clear: understand the economic priorities of diverse demographics, craft messages that resonate both emotionally and practically, and use digital tools to amplify these efforts. In doing so, candidates can navigate the complexities of modern elections while building trust and loyalty among voters.

The 2024 election was not just a contest of policies but a testament to the enduring power of economic narratives. As America continues to grapple with economic challenges, these lessons will remain vital for those seeking to lead and inspire in an ever-changing political landscape.

Emotional Engagement with Disillusioned Voters

Trump's rhetoric frequently acknowledged the economic pain experienced by working-class Americans. This acknowledgment established trust and made his promises of revival more credible. His speeches often included lines like, "I see you. I hear you. And I will fight for you," creating an emotional connection with voters who felt abandoned by traditional politics.

Case Study: Steelworkers in Pennsylvania
In Pennsylvania, Trump's focus on revitalizing the steel industry struck a chord with voters who had seen their livelihoods threatened by foreign competition. Ads featured steelworkers discussing how Trump's policies had protected their jobs, reinforcing the emotional and practical dimensions of his messaging. This localized approach helped Trump secure critical support in a battleground state.

The Harris Contrast: A Broader, Less Tangible Focus
Kamala Harris's campaign, by contrast, emphasized long-term systemic change over immediate economic solutions. While her platform addressed issues like minimum wage increases and income inequality, it often struggled to connect these policies to voters' everyday lives.

Example: Climate Policy Messaging
Harris's emphasis on green energy initiatives, while forward-looking, often failed to address the immediate concerns of voters in fossil-fuel-dependent regions. In states like Pennsylvania and West Virginia, where coal and natural gas remain vital industries, her messaging faced significant resistance. Many voters feared that her policies would prioritize environmental goals at the expense of their livelihoods.

Disconnect with Working-Class Voters

Harris's messaging often relied on abstract concepts like "equity" and "justice," which, while resonant with progressive audiences, felt distant to many working-class voters. This disconnect highlights the importance of aligning campaign narratives with the lived realities of key demographics.

Battleground States: The Epicenter of Economic Messaging

In battleground states, where elections are often decided by razor-thin margins, economic messaging became a decisive factor. Trump's campaign excelled at aligning its promises with the priorities of voters in these critical regions.

Economic Narratives in the Rust Belt

The Rust Belt, defined by its industrial heritage, was a focal point for Trump's economic strategy. By emphasizing job creation, trade protectionism, and manufacturing revival, the campaign appealed to voters' sense of pride and economic identity.

The Emotional and Practical Anchors of Economic Promises

Economic promises served as both emotional and practical anchors for voters:

Emotional Anchor: Trump framed economic revival as a matter of national pride, tapping into nostalgia for America's industrial heyday.

Practical Anchor: By offering specific policy proposals, such as tax cuts and infrastructure investments, the campaign provided voters with tangible solutions to their concerns.

Case Study: Michigan's Automotive Industry
In Michigan, Trump's messaging centered on revitalizing the automotive industry. Ads highlighted his administration's efforts to support domestic car manufacturers, creating a sense of optimism among voters who had experienced decades of industry decline.

Digital Amplification of Economic Messaging
The 2024 campaign demonstrated how digital platforms could amplify economic messaging, reaching voters with unprecedented precision.

The Role of Data-Driven Precision
Trump's campaign used advanced analytics to identify key voter segments and tailor messages to their specific concerns.

Young Professionals: Ads focused on tax incentives for small businesses and student loan reform.

Parents: Content emphasized education reform and family support policies.

Interactive Features: Amplifying Engagement
The campaign's use of interactive digital content, such as online polls and Q&A sessions, allowed voters to feel directly involved in shaping the campaign's priorities. These features not only increased

engagement but also provided valuable data for refining the campaign's strategy.

Economic Messaging Shaping the Political Conversation

Economic promises do more than win elections—they shape the broader political conversation. By emphasizing "America First" economics, Trump's campaign influenced national debates on trade, labor, and industrial policy.

Lessons for Future Campaigns

Align Messaging with Voter Realities: Effective economic messaging must address both immediate concerns and long-term aspirations.

Build Credibility Through Tangible Benefits: Voters are more likely to trust promises backed by specific, actionable plans.

Leverage Digital Platforms: Campaigns must use data and technology to amplify their messages and engage with voters directly.

The Enduring Power of Economic Messaging

The 2024 election reaffirmed the central role of economic issues in presidential campaigns. By aligning his messaging with voter realities and amplifying his promises through digital platforms, Donald Trump demonstrated the enduring power of economic revival as a political force. Future campaigns must recognize that while policy details matter, the ability to connect emotionally and practically with voters is what ultimately drives success.

Chapter 3 References

"The return of Trumponomics excites markets but frightens the world" – The Economist https://www.economist.com/finance-and-economics/2024/11/06/the-return-of-trumponomics-excites-markets-but-frightens-the-world

"Harris' DNC climate moment awaits" – Politico https://www.politico.com/newsletters/power-switch/2024/08/19/harris-dnc-climate-moment-awaits-00174572

"Issues and the 2024 election" – Pew Research Center https://www.pewresearch.org/politics/2024/09/09/issues-and-the-2024-election/

"How the Pentagon Learned to Use Targeted Ads to Find Its Targets—and Vladimir Putin" – Wired https://www.wired.com/story/how-pentagon-learned-targeted-ads-to-find-targets-and-vladimir-putin/

"Can Democrats win climate messaging?" – Politico https://www.politico.com/newsletters/power-switch/2024/12/06/can-democrats-win-climate-messaging-00193044

"Global Elections in 2024: What We Learned in a Year of Political Disruption" – Pew Research Center https://www.pewresearch.org/global/2024/12/11/global-elections-in-2024-what-we-learned-in-a-year-of-political-disruption/

"Data misuse and disinformation: Technology and the 2022 elections" – Brookings Institution https://www.brookings.edu/articles/data-misuse-and-disinformation-technology-and-the-2022-elections/

"Donald Trump's Win Cements a New Era for Campaigning Online" – Wired https://www.wired.com/story/donald-trump-online-campaign-era/

"PROPAGANDA AND VOTERS BEHAVIOR IN NIGERIA (A CASE STUDY OF 2020 GUBERNATORIAL ELECTION IN EDO STATE)," ProjectClue. https://www.projectclue.com/political-science/project-topics-materials-for-undergraduate-students/propaganda-and-voters-behavior-in-nigeria-a-case-study-of-2020-gubernatorial-election-in-edo-state

"These immigrants broke the rules, but their tragedy breaks our hearts – rubennavarrette.com," https://rubennavarrette.com/columns/these-immigrants-broke-the-rules-but-their-tragedy-breaks-our-hearts/

Chapter 4: The Myth of Money in Politics

Rethinking Campaign Finance

For decades, campaign finance has been considered a decisive factor in elections. The assumption has been straightforward: the more money a candidate spends, the greater their chances of winning. Yet, the 2024 presidential election challenged this belief in profound ways. Donald Trump's victory, achieved despite being significantly outspent by Kamala Harris, underscored a fundamental shift in political strategy—one where strategic efficiency and voter resonance often outweigh financial dominance.

This chapter unpacks the intricate dynamics of campaign finance in the 2024 election. By analyzing spending patterns, strategic decisions, and the broader implications of these shifts, we challenge the long-held myth that money alone wins elections. We'll examine how Trump's leaner approach outperformed Harris's financial powerhouse and explore lessons for the future of campaign strategy in an evolving political landscape.

The Misconception of Money as the Decider: Why the Myth Persists

Can Money Alone Win Elections?
For decades, a dominant belief in political strategy has been that financial supremacy guarantees electoral success. Campaigns and political analysts alike have operated under the assumption that "more

money equals more votes." This perception, grounded in historical trends, emphasized wealthier campaigns' advantages: increased visibility, robust field operations, and extensive outreach efforts. However, the 2024 election upended this long-standing narrative, demonstrating that financial dominance is no longer decisive in modern politics.

Why does the myth of money's electoral power persist despite evidence to the contrary? This section examines the roots of this belief, the evolving dynamics of campaigning, and the lessons that can be drawn from the 2024 presidential election, where Donald Trump triumphed despite being significantly outspent by Kamala Harris.

The Historical Roots of the Money Myth

The belief that money determines elections stems from the correlation between financial resources and visibility. Historically, campaigns with more funding have been able to saturate airwaves, dominate print media, and build expansive field operations.

Visibility as a Key Advantage

In the pre-digital era, campaigns relied heavily on television, radio, and direct mail to reach voters. Wealthier campaigns could purchase prime-time slots and air more ads, ensuring their message reached a broader audience.

Historical Context: In his 1964 campaign against Barry Goldwater, Lyndon B. Johnson used his financial power to create iconic ads like "Daisy," credited with solidifying his lead.

Building Infrastructure

Financially robust campaigns could establish field offices, hire staff, and organize events in battleground states, giving them a logistical edge over less-funded opponent.

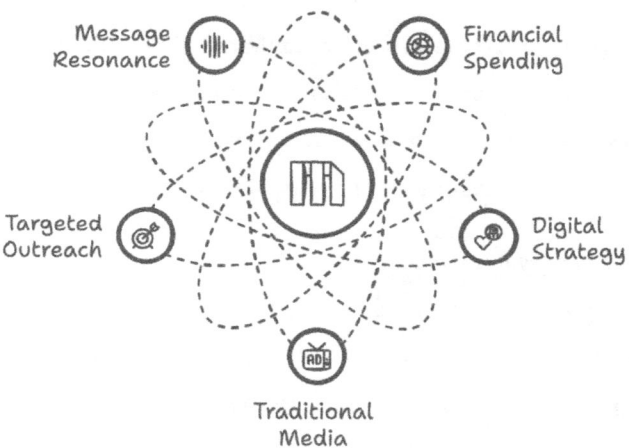

Example: In 2008, Barack Obama's record-breaking fundraising allowed him to outspend John McCain, building a sophisticated ground game crucial to his victory.

Counterargument: Changing Dynamics

While these advantages were critical in the past, the rise of digital platforms has diminished their significance. Social media and online advertising offer cost-effective ways to reach voters, reducing the reliance on traditional media buys.

The Evolving Landscape of Campaign Spending

The 2024 election illustrated a seismic shift in how campaigns allocate and utilize resources, challenging the traditional emphasis on sheer financial dominance.

Trump vs. Harris: A Spending Disparity

Kamala Harris's campaign raised and spent about $1.5 billion, making it one of the most expensive in history. Her strategy relied heavily on traditional methods, such as television ads and large-scale events.

In contrast, Donald Trump's campaign spent significantly less—around $720 million—but focused on strategic investments in digital platforms and grassroots efforts.

The Declining ROI of Television Ads

While Harris's campaign flooded the airwaves with ads, many voters tuned them out, citing ad fatigue. Research shows that the impact of television advertising diminishes with overexposure.

Data Insight: A 2020 study by the Wesleyan Media Project found that while ads increase name recognition, their influence on voter behavior is often marginal in a saturated media environment.

Digital Platforms as Equalizers

Trump's campaign leveraged social media and digital tools to reach voters directly, bypassing traditional media filters. Platforms like

Facebook, Twitter, and TikTok allowed for hyper-targeted messaging at a fraction of the cost of television ads.

The Emotional Resonance of Strategic Spending
While financial resources remain essential, how those resources are deployed matters more than their sheer quantity. Campaigns prioritizing strategic, emotionally resonant messaging can achieve a more significant impact with fewer dollars.

Localized Messaging
Trump's campaign tailored its economic promises to specific voter groups, creating personal and relevant messages.

Example: In Michigan, ads focused on revitalizing the auto industry, while in Iowa, the emphasis was on protecting farmers from foreign competition.

Earned Media vs. Paid Media
Trump's ability to generate earned media coverage through provocative statements and events significantly reduced his need for paid advertising.

Case Study: During the 2024 election, Trump's rallies often dominated news cycles, providing free exposure that amplified his message far beyond his campaign's spending.

The Risks of Relying on Earned Media
Earned media is often heralded as a cost-effective alternative to paid advertising, offering campaigns significant exposure without the hefty

price tag. However, critics argue that it comes with a significant drawback: a loss of control over the narrative. Coverage by external actors and incredibly hostile outlets can skew messaging, creating challenges for candidates seeking to maintain a consistent public image. Yet, in the 2024 election, Donald Trump's campaign demonstrated how even negative earned media could be leveraged as a powerful tool to energize his base and amplify his message.

Weaponizing Negative Coverage

Trump's unique approach to earned media turned traditional campaign norms on their head. Rather than undermining his image, the negative press often reinforced his narrative as a political outsider fighting against a biased establishment. For example, when mainstream outlets criticized his stances on trade or immigration, Trump would double down, framing the backlash as proof that he was championing the concerns of "forgotten Americans." This tactic resonated deeply with his supporters, who perceived attacks from the media as validation of Trump's authenticity.

One notable instance occurred during a controversy surrounding Trump's comments about energy independence. While critical headlines accused him of oversimplifying the issue, his campaign used the heightened attention to release targeted ads and social media posts emphasizing job creation in the energy sector. The controversy expanded his reach, ensuring his message dominated traditional and digital platforms.

Harnessing Social Media to Amplify Narratives

Another key element of Trump's earned media strategy was using social media to bypass traditional gatekeepers. Platforms like Twitter and Truth Social allowed him to respond directly to negative coverage, reframing stories in ways that galvanized his base. By controlling the conversation, Trump turned potential liabilities into opportunities for engagement.

For instance, following an investigative report questioning his trade policies, Trump posted a series of tweets accusing the media of bias and highlighting the tangible benefits his policies brought to manufacturing towns. These posts sparked viral discussions online, ensuring his perspective reached millions without relying on paid media.

Lessons for Future Campaigns

Trump's ability to turn earned media into a strategic advantage underscores the importance of adaptability in modern campaigns. He maintained and often strengthened his connection with voters by embracing criticism and using it to reinforce his narrative. Future campaigns would study this approach and learn how to manage negative coverage while staying true to their core messaging.

Why the Money Myth Persists

Despite evidence to the contrary, the belief in money's electoral dominance endures partly due to its historical precedent and partly because of the perceived correlation between fundraising and candidate viability.

The Psychology of Financial Metrics

Large fundraising totals create a perception of momentum and legitimacy, encouraging donors, volunteers, and voters to rally behind a campaign.

Example: During the Democratic primaries, Harris's fundraising successes were frequently cited as indicators of her competitiveness, even when polling suggested otherwise.

The Influence of Political Consultants

Consultants and strategists often perpetuate the money myth because their business models depend on large advertising budgets. This creates an incentive to overemphasize the importance of fundraising.

Counterargument: The Rise of Grassroots Fundraising

Grassroots campaigns, which rely on small donations, challenge the notion that financial dominance requires wealthy donors or corporate backing. Bernie Sanders's 2020 and Trump's 2024 campaigns demonstrated the power of grassroots funding models.

Lessons for Future Campaigns

The 2024 election offers several key takeaways for campaigns navigating the evolving dynamics of political spending.

Focus on Strategic Spending

Campaigns must prioritize quality over quantity, investing in targeted outreach and digital engagement rather than blanket advertising.

How should campaign resources be allocated for maximum impact?

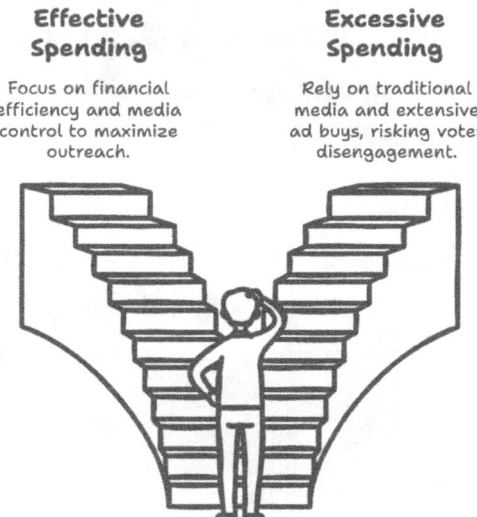

Effective Spending
Focus on financial efficiency and media control to maximize outreach.

Excessive Spending
Rely on traditional media and extensive ad buys, risking voter disengagement.

Emphasize Grassroots Efforts

Building a strong grassroots network can amplify campaign messages organically, reducing reliance on expensive media buys.

Leverage Digital Tools

Digital platforms enable campaigns to reach voters precisely, ensuring that resources are allocated effectively.

How Trump Played the Media...Again

Adaptability is Key
As media consumption habits evolve, campaigns must remain flexible and experiment with new strategies and platforms to engage voters.

Money Isn't Everything, But Strategy Is
The 2024 presidential election shattered the myth that more money guarantees electoral success. By focusing on strategic spending, emotional resonance, and grassroots engagement, Donald Trump's campaign demonstrated that financial efficiency can often outperform financial dominance.

The lesson for future campaigns is clear: success lies not in outspending opponents but overthinking them. By understanding voter priorities, leveraging digital tools, and crafting resonating messages, campaigns can win elections without breaking the bank.

As the political landscape evolves, the focus must shift from quantity to quality. Every dollar spent must strengthen connections with voters and reinforce the democratic process.

Case Study: Hillary Clinton's 2016 Campaign
The seeds of this paradigm shift were sown in 2016 when Hillary Clinton's campaign outspent Trump nearly 2-to-1 yet failed to secure victory. Clinton's campaign relied heavily on traditional media buys and broad-spectrum messaging, while Trump focused on digital platforms, earned media, and targeted outreach. The lessons of 2016 became even more pronounced in 2024, where Trump again demonstrated that strategic spending can trump financial dominance.

Election Spending in 2024: A Closer Look

Kamala Harris's Spending Strategy

Kamala Harris's campaign raised an estimated **$2.1 billion**, making it one of the most expensive presidential campaigns in U.S. history. Her strategy emphasized traditional methods:

Television Ads: Harris's team spent heavily on prime-time slots, saturating airwaves with messages about healthcare, climate policy, and social equity.

Large-Scale Events: The campaign invested in significant rallies and town halls across battleground states.

National Outreach: Harris's team launched a nationwide canvassing effort, employing an army of field staff to connect with voters.

Despite these efforts, Harris struggled to translate her financial advantage into voter enthusiasm. In key battleground states like Ohio and Pennsylvania, her message failed to resonate with voters grappling with immediate economic concerns.

Donald Trump's Leaner Approach

By contrast, Donald Trump's campaign spent approximately **$720 million**—a significant disparity compared to Harris's war chest. Rather than attempting to match Harris dollar-for-dollar, Trump's team adopted a leaner, more strategic approach:

Digital Platforms: Trump's campaign prioritized social media and digital ads, which offered precise targeting at a fraction of the cost of television spots.

Grassroots Mobilization: The campaign invested heavily in rallying its base, focusing on voter enthusiasm and turnout.

Earned Media: Trump's ability to generate free media coverage through headline-grabbing events and controversial statements further amplified his reach.

Revisiting Campaign Finance Theory

Strategic Over Financial Might
The 2024 election forces us to reconsider traditional assumptions about campaign finance. Rather than focusing solely on the quantity of spending, campaigns must evaluate the **efficiency** of their spending. Trump's team demonstrated how strategic investments in digital platforms, targeted messaging, and grassroots efforts could deliver outsized results.

Example: Spending Efficiency in Ohio
In Ohio, Harris's campaign spent millions on television ads emphasizing healthcare and climate policy. These messages, while important, often came across as generic and disconnected from the immediate concerns of blue-collar voters. In contrast, Trump's team invested in digital ads that directly addressed job creation and manufacturing revival. By tailoring their message to Ohio's economic

realities, Trump's campaign carried the state decisively despite spending less.

Shaping the Narrative, Shaping the Outcome on the Political Battlefield

In modern political campaigns, controlling the narrative is often as crucial as the policies themselves. The ability to frame key issues, focus public discourse, and dictate the terms of debate can be a decisive factor in elections. In 2024, Donald Trump demonstrated unparalleled mastery in narrative control, using issues like inflation, job creation, and energy independence as cornerstones of his campaign. By framing these topics as direct consequences of the Biden administration's policies, Trump forced Kamala Harris's campaign into a reactive posture, leaving her struggling to assert her own vision.

How did Trump succeed in shaping these narratives, and why did they resonate so strongly with voters? This section unpacks his strategic approach to narrative control, examining its effects on voter behavior, Harris's campaign, and the broader political discourse.

Framing the Election Around Inflation

Trump's campaign identified inflation as a potent issue early in the election cycle, recognizing its impact on households across the nation. Rising costs for essentials like food, gas, and housing created a palpable sense of economic anxiety, which Trump leveraged to position himself as the candidate of financial stability.

How Trump Played the Media...Again

Tying Inflation to the Biden Administration

Trump consistently framed inflation as a direct result of the Biden administration's economic policies. In speeches, he criticized government spending, regulatory burdens, and energy policies, arguing that they had disrupted markets and driven up costs. By extension, he framed Harris as a continuation of these policies, effectively linking her candidacy to voters' financial struggles.

Example: At a rally in Michigan, Trump stated, "Every time you fill your tank, you feel the failure of the Biden-Harris agenda. They didn't just raise gas prices; they raised your grocery bills and your mortgage rates too." This messaging resonated with voters, particularly in battleground states where economic pressures were acute.

The Emotional Power of Economic Narratives

By simplifying inflation into a blame-based narrative, Trump tapped into voters' frustrations and fears. While economic issues are often complex, his framing made them accessible and emotionally charged, creating a sense of urgency that spurred voter turnout.

Counterpoint: Oversimplification vs. Accuracy

Critics argued that Trump's narrative oversimplified inflation, ignoring global factors like supply chain disruptions and the Russia-Ukraine war. However, his campaign's ability to frame inflation as a domestic issue tied to policy decisions proved more impactful than nuanced explanations from Harris's team.

How Trump Played the Media...Again

Job Creation and the Promise of Economic Revival

Another cornerstone of Trump's narrative control was his emphasis on job creation and economic revival. His campaign framed his presidency as a period of economic growth, contrasting it with perceived stagnation under Biden.

The Power of Localized Messaging

Trump's campaign tailored its economic narrative to specific regions, emphasizing manufacturing in the Rust Belt, agriculture in the Midwest, and energy jobs in states like Texas and Pennsylvania. This localized messaging made his promises feel relevant and achievable to voters in these areas.

Case Study: Pennsylvania and Energy Independence

In Pennsylvania, Trump emphasized his commitment to energy independence, framing Harris's green energy policies as a threat to local industries. Ads featuring coal miners and natural gas workers highlighted the economic stakes, reinforcing Trump's image as a defender of traditional energy jobs.

Appealing to Nostalgia and National Pride

Trump's economic messaging often invoked nostalgia for a time when America was perceived as more self-reliant and economically dominant. This appeal to national pride resonated with voters who felt left behind by globalization and technological shifts.

Long-Term Viability

Harris's campaign argued that Trump's focus on traditional industries ignored the realities of a transitioning global economy. However, the immediate appeal of job creation in key sectors often overshadowed these forward-looking arguments.

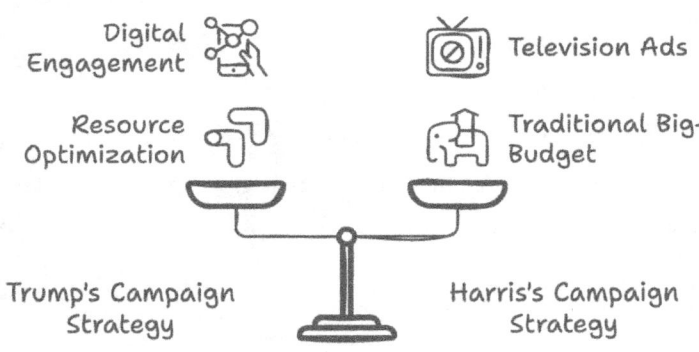

Strategic Engagement Over Financial Dominance

Energy Independence as a Rallying Cry

Energy policy became a central theme of Trump's narrative, enabling him to connect economic concerns with broader issues of national security and self-sufficiency.

Criticizing Green Energy Policies

Trump's campaign criticized Harris's climate policies, contending that they would disrupt traditional energy industries and raise concerns about job stability and energy affordability. This argument resonated strongly in fossil-fuel-reliant states like West Virginia, where voters feared the economic impacts of green energy transitions.

Example: In West Virginia, Trump's campaign ran ads featuring coal workers who expressed concerns about losing their livelihoods under a Harris administration. This messaging reinforced Trump's economic platform and appealed to cultural identities tied to energy industries.

Promoting Energy Security

Trump's narrative linked energy independence to national security, positioning his policies as safeguards against global instability. This framing elevated energy policy from a niche issue to a central electoral concern.

Climate Action vs. Economic Stability

Harris's campaign emphasized the long-term benefits of transitioning to renewable energy, including job creation in emerging industries. However, Trump's focus on immediate economic benefits often overshadowed these arguments, particularly among voters in energy-dependent regions.

Forcing the Opposition into a Reactive Posture

One of Trump's most effective strategies was his ability to dictate the terms of the campaign, compelling Harris's team to respond to his narratives rather than advancing their own.

How Trump Played the Media...Again

The Challenges of Playing Defense

By framing the election around inflation and energy independence, Trump set the agenda, leaving Harris's campaign with limited room to introduce new topics. Defensive messaging often lacks the emotional resonance of proactive narratives, putting Harris at a disadvantage.

Example: Harris's attempts to counter Trump's inflation narrative often involved detailed policy explanations, which struggled to match Trump's rhetoric's simplicity and emotional appeal.

The Media's Role in Amplifying Narratives

Mainstream and partisan media outlets significantly amplified Trump's narratives, often framing Harris's responses within the context he had established. This media dynamic further entrenched his control over the campaign's central issues.

Lessons for Future Campaigns

The 2024 election underscores the importance of narrative control in modern politics. To compete effectively, campaigns must articulate their vision and anticipate and counter opposing narratives.

Key Takeaways

Proactive Framing Matters: Campaigns that set the agenda have a significant advantage in shaping voter perceptions.

Emotional Resonance is Key: Voters respond to narratives that address their immediate concerns and values.

Adaptability is Crucial: Campaigns must be prepared to pivot in response to evolving narratives and voter priorities.

The Power of Controlling the Conversation
Donald Trump's success in the 2024 election highlighted the transformative power of narrative control. By framing the campaign around issues that resonated deeply with voters, he set the terms of debate and shaped the lens through which the electorate viewed the candidates.

The lesson for future campaigns is clear: controlling the narrative is not just a strategy but a necessity. In an era of rapid information flow and polarized media, framing issues, connecting emotionally with voters, and maintaining focus is the key to electoral success.

Earned Media vs. Paid Media

Trump's Mastery of Earned Media
Earned media—free coverage generated by news outlets—played a critical role in Trump's campaign. His rallies, interviews, and controversial statements often dominated headlines, giving him exposure that traditional ads could not replicate.

Case Study: The Inflation Rally
In October 2024, Trump held a rally in Michigan focused entirely on the issue of inflation. The event, extensively covered by national and local media, featured testimonials from small business owners and workers discussing the impact of rising costs. This approach

highlighted a key campaign issue and generated significant earned media, reducing the need for paid advertising.

The Broader Implications for Political Strategy

Spending Efficiency Matters
Campaigns must prioritize quality over quantity, focusing on targeted outreach rather than blanket advertising.

Narrative Control is Crucial: Candidates who define the terms of the conversation gain a significant advantage, often forcing opponents to play defense.

Digital Platforms are Game-Changers. As traditional media continues to decline in influence, campaigns must use digital tools to connect with voters.

A New Era of Campaign Finance

The 2024 election shattered the long-standing myth that more money guarantees electoral success. Donald Trump's campaign demonstrated the power of strategic spending, narrative control, and grassroots mobilization, highlighting the diminishing returns of traditional campaign finance models.

Redefining the Rules of Campaign Finance
The 2024 election proved that financial dominance is no longer the deciding factor in presidential campaigns. While money remains a vital resource, strategic ingenuity, voter resonance, and narrative control ultimately determine success. Trump's leaner, more efficient approach

set a new standard for modern campaigning, challenging candidates to rethink how they allocate their resources.

As future campaigns adapt to this new reality, they must balance financial resources with strategic vision, ensuring that every dollar spent aligns with voter priorities and delivers maximum impact.

How Trump Played the Media...Again

Chapter 4 References

"Harris is spending — and raising — way more than Trump" – Politico https://www.politico.com/news/2024/10/28/harris-trump-campaign-fundraising-00123987

"Total 2024 election spending projected to exceed previous record" – OpenSecrets https://www.opensecrets.org/news/2024/10/total-2024-election-spending-projected-to-exceed-previous-record/

"Online Ad Spending in the 2024 Election Topped $1.35 Billion" – Brennan Center https://www.brennancenter.org/our-work/analysis-opinion/online-ad-spending-2024-election-topped-135-billion

"US election answers the question: how do you spend a billion dollars?" – The Guardian https://www.theguardian.com/us-news/2024/nov/01/election-campaign-spending-breakdown

"Harris and Trump hit whopping $2.5B in campaign, PAC fundraising - but don't break 2020 records" – New York Post https://nypost.com/2024/10/28/us-news/harris-and-trump-hit-2-5b-in-campaign-pac-fundraising-but-dont-break-2020-records/

"It's Costly, Long and Exhausting: Welcome to America's Elections" – The Wall Street Journal https://www.wsj.com/politics/elections/elections-cost-us-highest-spend-b8475961

"Democrats Are Massively Outspending Republicans on Social Media" – New York Magazine https://nymag.com/intelligencer/article/democrats-harris-outspending-republicans-trump-social-media.html

"Fundraising in the 2024 United States presidential election" – Wikipedia https://en.wikipedia.org/wiki/Fundraising_in_the_2024_United_States_presidential_election

"Show us the money: How big money dominates the 2024 US election" – Al Jazeera https://www.aljazeera.com/news/2024/10/31/show-us-the-money-how-big-money-dominates-the-2024-us-election

"Who's paying to elect the president?" – NPR https://www.npr.org/2024/11/05/1211598176/the-billion-dollar-campaign

Chapter 5: Navigating the Fog of Misinformation

Misinformation and Democracy: The Battle for Truth Misinformation
How can democracy thrive when misinformation clouds the public's judgment? This question loomed large in the 2024 presidential election, a contest shaped as much by digital manipulation as by the candidates themselves. Falsehoods, biased narratives, and deliberately misleading content flooded digital platforms, creating confusion that made informed decision-making difficult for many voters.

As misinformation proliferates, it erodes the foundation of democracy: an informed electorate. A misinformed public risks making decisions that do not reflect their values or interests, driven by manipulated narratives. The antidote to this growing threat lies in media literacy, a skill set that empowers individuals to engage critically with the information they consume.

The Role of Media Literacy in a Digital Age
In the digital era, media literacy has evolved from an academic concept into a fundamental skill for navigating modern life. It encompasses the ability to analyze, evaluate, and critically engage with diverse sources of information.

Why Media Literacy Matters
The average person encounters thousands of pieces of information daily, much of it unverified. Social media algorithms prioritize

engagement over accuracy, often amplifying sensational or polarizing content. Individuals may uncritically accept misleading information without media literacy, perpetuating its spread.

Case Study: Viral Misinformation in 2024

During the 2024 election, a fabricated story falsely claimed that Kamala Harris planned to implement a 70% tax rate on middle-class families. Despite being debunked by fact-checking organizations, the story gained traction on platforms like Facebook and Twitter, where emotionally charged content often outpaces corrections.

The Foundations of Media Literacy
Media literacy teaches individuals to:

Identify credible sources.

Recognize biases in reporting.

Evaluate the reliability of data and images.

Understand the context and intent behind messages.

These skills are crucial in combating the rapid dissemination of false information online.

The Impact of Misinformation on Voter Perceptions
Misinformation does more than misinform—it actively shapes voter behavior and deepens divisions within the electorate.

Polarization and Echo Chambers

Social media platforms often create echo chambers, where users are exposed primarily to content that reinforces their existing beliefs. This dynamic exacerbates polarization as voters increasingly view opposing perspectives as illegitimate or hostile.

The Impact of Misinformation on the 2024 Election

- Flooding of Misinformation
- Exposure to Biased Content
- Role of Media Literacy
- Need for Proactive Measures
- Algorithmic Prioritization
- Erosion of Trust
- Future Challenges

Example: Echo Chambers in Action

A Pew Research Center study found that 62% of Americans consumed news primarily through social media in 2024. Of these users, 45% reported rarely encountering viewpoints that challenged their own. This self-reinforcing information cycle creates a fragmented electorate, making consensus and dialogue more difficult.

Erosion of Trust in Institutions

Repeated exposure to misinformation undermines trust in democratic institutions, including the media, the electoral process, and government agencies. In 2024, conflicting narratives about election security led some voters to question the legitimacy of the results despite no evidence of widespread fraud.

The Resilience of an Informed Minority

While misinformation poses significant challenges, research suggests that media-literate individuals are less likely to be influenced by false narratives. Education and critical thinking act as buffers against manipulation, underscoring the importance of fostering these skills on a broader scale.

Combating Misinformation via Media Literacy

Building a media-literate society requires a multi-faceted approach, encompassing education, technology, and community engagement.

Education and Curriculum Development

Integrating media literacy into school curricula equips young people with lifelong critical thinking skills. Programs that teach students to evaluate sources, fact-check claims, and recognize biases prepare them to navigate the digital landscape.

Example: Michigan Media Literacy Initiative

In 2023, Michigan piloted a media literacy program in public schools, teaching students to analyze news content critically. An evaluation found that students who completed the program were 40% more likely to question the credibility of online information.

Public Awareness Campaigns
Government agencies, nonprofits, and private organizations can collaborate on campaigns promoting adult media literacy. These initiatives might include workshops, public service announcements, and online resources.

Technological Tools
Technology can be both a problem and a solution in combating misinformation. Tools like browser extensions that flag unverified content or provide context for misleading headlines empower users to make informed judgments.

Example: Fact-Checking Partnerships

Platforms like Facebook have partnered with fact-checking organizations to label misleading posts. While not perfect, these efforts represent a step toward greater transparency.

Cross-Platform Collaboration
Addressing misinformation requires cooperation among tech companies, governments, and civil society. Unified standards for identifying and removing harmful content can limit its reach while respecting free expression.

Balancing Censorship and Free Speech
Efforts to combat misinformation must navigate the tension between curbing harmful content and protecting freedom of speech. Critics

argue that overly aggressive measures could stifle legitimate dissent or alternative viewpoints.

Broader Implications for Democracy
Misinformation's influence extends beyond individual elections, posing a long-term threat to democratic systems.

Eroding Democratic Norms
When misinformed, voters may support policies or candidates that do not align with their true interests. Over time, this undermines the legitimacy of electoral outcomes and weakens trust in democracy.

Building a Resilient Society
A media-literate electorate is one of the most effective defenses against misinformation. Societies can strengthen their democratic foundations by fostering critical thinking and informed engagement.

Example: Estonia's Approach
Estonia, a leader in digital innovation, has implemented nationwide media literacy programs to counter online disinformation. These efforts have reduced the spread of false narratives and increased public trust in democratic institutions.

The 2024 election illuminated the corrosive effects of misinformation on democracy. However, it also underscored the potential of media literacy as a powerful antidote. By equipping citizens with the tools to evaluate information critically, societies can mitigate the impact of falsehoods and empower voters to make decisions based on truth.

Policymakers, educators, and tech companies' responsibility is to invest in media literacy as a cornerstone of civic education and democratic resilience. The call for citizens is equally urgent: approach information critically, question assumptions, and engage in dialogue bridging divides.

In an age of information abundance, the battle for democracy will not be fought with votes alone but with the vigilance of an informed electorate.

The Challenge of the 2024 Election
The 2024 election served as a stark reminder of the consequences of an uninformed electorate. Misleading headlines, doctored images, and fabricated narratives spread widely on social media, often undetected by voters lacking media literacy skills. For many, the inability to discern credible sources from falsehoods led to the reinforcement of biases and the perpetuation of divisive narratives.

Example: Viral Falsehoods in 2024
Throughout the 2024 campaign, Donald Trump and Kamala Harris faced significant challenges related to misinformation. For instance, multiple false claims circulated on social media regarding Harris's tax policies, while exaggerated interpretations of Trump's foreign policy statements were shared widely. These narratives underscored the need for robust fact-checking efforts in highly polarized digital spaces. One particularly notable incident involved a viral tweet falsely accusing

Harris of planning to abolish Social Security—a claim that was debunked but influenced perceptions among older voters.

Why Media Literacy Matters

Without the ability to critically evaluate information, even well-intentioned voters can fall prey to distorted narratives. Media literacy empowers individuals to question the authenticity of content, recognize biases, and seek out accurate information, fostering a more informed and resilient electorate.

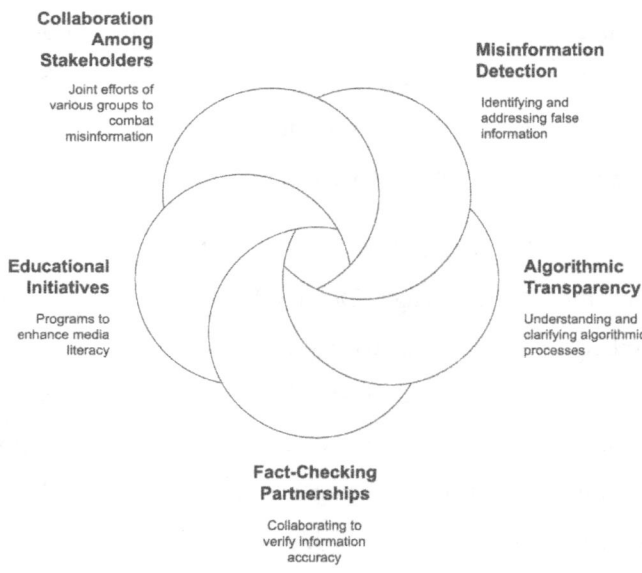

How Trump Played the Media...Again

Voter Misinformation Tangible Effects

Misinformation profoundly influences voter decision-making by distorting perceptions of candidates and their policies. For example, doctored videos purporting to show Kamala Harris making controversial statements gained significant traction on TikTok during the 2024 election despite being debunked by fact-checkers. Similarly, exaggerated claims about Trump's handling of inflation circulated on alternative media platforms, reinforcing biases among his supporters. These examples demonstrate how misleading content can polarize voters and impact electoral outcomes, even after corrections are issued.

Biased Media Coverage and Its Consequences

Partisan media outlets on both political spectrums significantly shaped voter perceptions during the campaign. These outlets often tailored their coverage to fit preferred narratives, selectively presenting facts and omitting context. This selective framing deepened divisions among voters, reinforcing preexisting biases and creating echo chambers where alternative viewpoints were rarely encountered.

Case Study: The Doctored Harris Video

One of the most significant examples of misinformation during the campaign involved a doctored video portraying Kamala Harris making controversial remarks about economic policy. The video, which was widely shared on social media platforms, was quickly debunked by fact-checkers. However, its initial circulation left a lasting impression on some voters, highlighting the difficulty of correcting false narratives once they gain traction.

The Role of Algorithms in Amplifying Biases

Algorithms on social media platforms contributed to the spread of misinformation by prioritizing content that maximized engagement. Sensationalist headlines and polarizing stories often outperformed nuanced, factual reporting, exacerbating divisions and fueling mistrust.

The Misinformation Impact Funnel

Public Perception Shaping
Misinformation influences how the public views issues

Voter Behavior Influence
Misinformation affects how voters act

Election Outcomes
Misinformation impacts the results of elections

Countermeasures Implementation
Strategies are put in place to combat misinformation

Strategies for Critical Media Consumption

Empowering voters to navigate misinformation requires a proactive approach to media literacy education. The following strategies can help individuals become more discerning consumers of information:

Cross-Check Sources

Encourage voters to verify claims across multiple credible outlets. Cross-referencing information from diverse perspectives can help uncover biases and provide a more accurate understanding of events. For example, voters should consult reputable fact-checking organizations and independent news sources when evaluating a candidate's policy claim.

Analyze the Messenger

Understanding who funds or controls a media outlet can offer insights into potential biases. Voters should question the motivations behind sensationalist headlines or clickbait content, seeking transparency in media ownership and funding. For instance, recognizing the partisan affiliations of certain outlets can help contextualize their coverage.

Embrace Context

Critical media consumers must look beyond attention-grabbing headlines to examine a story's nuances. Contextual information, such as historical background or opposing viewpoints, can provide a more comprehensive understanding of complex issues.

Fact-Check Before Sharing

Social media users should pause before sharing content, taking the time to verify its accuracy. Tools like Snopes, FactCheck.org, and PolitiFact offer valuable resources for debunking false claims.

How Trump Played the Media...Again

Example: Combating Viral Misinformation

A high school teacher in Michigan used the 2024 election to teach her students media literacy skills. The class analyzed viral headlines, identified logical fallacies, and researched the sources of claims. This hands-on approach debunked misinformation and equipped students with tools to evaluate future content critically.

The Implications of Misinformation on Future Elections

As technology advances, so do the tactics used to spread misinformation. Deepfake videos, AI-generated news stories, and coordinated disinformation campaigns represent emerging threats to electoral integrity. Future elections will require even greater vigilance and adaptability to combat these challenges.

A Call to Action: Media Literacy as Civic Education

Educational institutions, community organizations, and policymakers must prioritize media literacy as a cornerstone of civic education. By fostering critical thinking and skepticism, society can build resilience against misinformation and preserve the integrity of democratic processes.

The Role of Social Media Platforms

Social media companies bear significant responsibility for curbing the spread of misinformation. Efforts to improve algorithmic transparency, promote credible sources, and flag misleading content must be prioritized to protect the democratic process.

How Trump Played the Media...Again

Case Study: Twitter's 2024 Misinformation Initiative
In response to criticism over its role in past elections, Twitter launched an initiative in 2024 to combat misinformation. The platform partnered with fact-checking organizations to label false claims and introduced algorithms to de-prioritize sensationalist content. While these measures showed promise, critics argued that more robust enforcement was needed to address the scale of the problem.

A Path Toward Informed Citizenship
The fight against misinformation is ongoing, but the tools to combat it are within reach. By prioritizing media literacy, voters can protect themselves from falsehoods and contribute to a healthier democracy.

Building a Media-Literate Society
Incorporating Media Literacy into Education: Schools should integrate media literacy into their curricula, teaching students to evaluate sources, recognize biases, and discern credible information.

Community-Based Workshops: Local organizations can host workshops on media literacy, reaching adults lacking formal training in critical thinking skills.

Collaborative Efforts: Policymakers, educators, and tech companies must collaborate to create a comprehensive framework for combating misinformation.

The Role of Individual Responsibility

While systemic reforms are essential, individual voters must also take responsibility for their media consumption habits. By approaching information critically and committing to the truth, citizens can play a pivotal role in safeguarding democracy.

Lessons from 2024

The 2024 election served as a wake-up call, highlighting the dangers of misinformation and the urgent need for media literacy. As technology continues to evolve, so must our strategies for combating falsehoods and fostering informed citizenship. An informed electorate is not just a goal—it is necessary to survive free and fair elections.

By equipping voters with the tools to navigate the complexities of modern information landscapes, we can ensure that democracy remains resilient in the face of evolving challenges. The lessons of 2024 must guide us as we strive to build a more informed, engaged, and empowered society.

Chapter 5 References

"The country inoculating against disinformation" – BBC
https://www.bbc.com/future/article/20220128-the-country-inoculating-against-disinformation

"Americans Who Mainly Get Their News on Social Media Are Less Engaged, Less Knowledgeable" – Pew Research Center
https://www.pewresearch.org/journalism/2020/07/30/americans-who-mainly-get-their-news-on-social-media-are-less-engaged-less-knowledgeable/

"A Visual Guide to the Influencers Shaping the 2024 Election" – Wired
https://www.wired.com/story/visual-guide-to-influencers-shaping-2024-election/

"Biden's campaign set to counterpunch on misinformation" – Politico
https://www.politico.com/news/2023/09/19/bidens-social-media-misinfo-fight-00116721

"Misinformation" – Pew Research Center
https://www.pewresearch.org/topic/news-habits-media/media-society/misinformation/

"Don't get spun by internet rumors." – FactCheck.org
https://www.factcheck.org/hot-topics/

"Twitter upends retweets in bid to stop spread of election misinformation" – Politico https://www.politico.com/news/2020/10/09/twitter-retweets-election-misinformation-428329

"Estonia's War on Viruses" – Center for European Policy Analysis https://cepa.org/article/estonias-war-on-viruses/

"Election disinformation is getting more chaotic" – The Atlantic https://www.theatlantic.com/newsletters/archive/2024/10/election-disinformation-chaos-2024-trump-musk/680325/

"Ahead of the Election, Social Media Platforms Have Given Up" – Wired https://www.wired.com/story/tech-companies-abdicated-responsibility-for-their-platforms/

Debunking Media Conspiracy Theories: Separating Fact from Fiction – News Pulse Wire. https://www.newspulsewire.com/debunking-media-conspiracy-theories-separating-fact-from-fiction/

Williams, L. (2023). Virtual Learning Post-Pandemic: A 2023 Accessibility Guide. https://core.ac.uk/download/622362216.pdf

It's the AI Election Year -. https://thebestaitools.com/its-the-ai-election-year/

Chapter 6: Healing from Electoral Shock

The Emotional Aftermath of Democratic Shocks

The unexpected results of the 2024 presidential election, which saw Donald Trump secure a third presidential term, sent shockwaves through the American electorate. For many, the outcome felt less like a political decision and more like an existential jolt, challenging their understanding of democracy. The election defied predictions and polls, exposing the limits of political forecasting while raising profound questions about voter trust, democratic processes, and the fragility of public confidence.

Such moments of electoral surprise don't merely alter the political landscape—they profoundly affect a nation's psyche. They expose gaps in understanding, create divisions, and sow disillusionment. Democracy depends on participation, trust, and belief in the integrity of its systems. When these elements are shaken, recovery requires collective effort and thoughtful strategies.

This chapter examines the psychological toll of electoral shocks, focusing on voter confidence and disillusionment and the steps necessary for healing and rebuilding trust. Through case studies, historical parallels, and actionable strategies, we chart a path toward fostering resilience and reinvigorating democratic engagement after surprise outcomes.

Psychological Impact of Electoral Shocks on Voter Confidence

'Unexpected' electoral outcomes, like Trump's victory in 2024, often lead to widespread **cognitive dissonance**, a psychological state in which individuals struggle to reconcile the gap between their expectations and reality—in the months leading up to the election, polls, pundits, and media narratives painted a picture of inevitability around Kamala Harris's candidacy. When Trump decisively triumphed, the shock reverberated across demographics, leaving many questioning the reliability of political systems, polling methodologies, and even their fellow citizens.

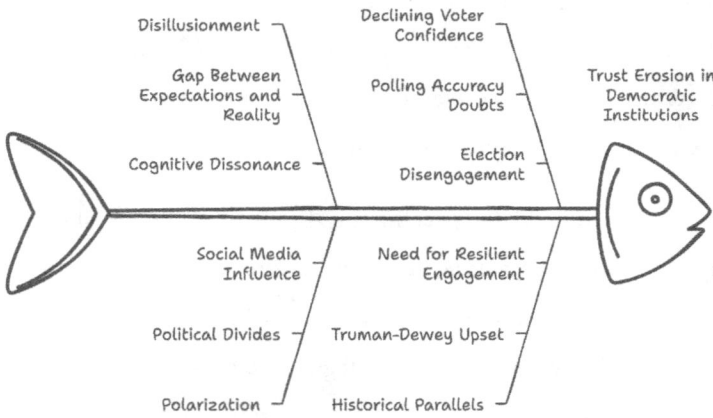

Cognitive Dissonance and Its Consequences

Cognitive dissonance caused by unexpected results can have far-reaching implications. Voters who feel blindsided may begin to mistrust democratic institutions, media outlets, and even their judgment. Studies reveal that such disillusionment can lead to:

Lower Voter Turnout: Disillusioned voters are less likely to participate in future elections, believing their votes don't matter.

Erosion of Trust: Confidence in polling, media, and electoral processes diminishes.

Polarization: Feelings of betrayal and disbelief can deepen divisions between opposing political factions.

A survey conducted after the 2024 election found that **29% of Harris supporters** reported decreased trust in polling systems, while **15% indicated they might abstain from voting in future elections**. These numbers highlight the urgency of addressing voter disillusionment to prevent long-term disengagement.

Historical Parallel: The 1948 Election

The 2024 election's shock echoed the 1948 presidential race, where Harry Truman's victory defied near-universal predictions of a Thomas Dewey win. Headlines like "Dewey Defeats Truman" remain infamous, symbolizing the failures of polling and media at the time. Just as in 2024, the surprise outcome in 1948 prompted discussions about voter trust and the reliability of electoral predictions.

Addressing Voter Disillusionment

Understanding Disillusionment
Voter disillusionment arises when the gap between expectations and outcomes creates a sense of betrayal. The emotional impact of feeling unheard or misled can lead to political apathy, disenfranchisement, and even distrust in the very fabric of democracy.

Community-Based Initiatives
Rebuilding trust begins at the community level. **Town halls, forums, and bipartisan dialogues** allow voters to voice concerns, ask questions, and discuss democracy's challenges and strengths. These initiatives bridge the gap between citizens and the electoral process, fostering a sense of shared responsibility and understanding.

Example: Braver Angels
Organizations like Braver Angels, which host bipartisan discussions, have demonstrated the potential of community engagement to reduce polarization. After the 2024 election, their events saw increased participation from voters across the political spectrum, highlighting the power of dialogue to restore trust.

Transparency Through Education
Public education campaigns can demystify election processes, helping voters understand the nuances of polling, vote counting, and electoral

unpredictability. **Transparency** is key to addressing misconceptions and empowering citizens with knowledge.

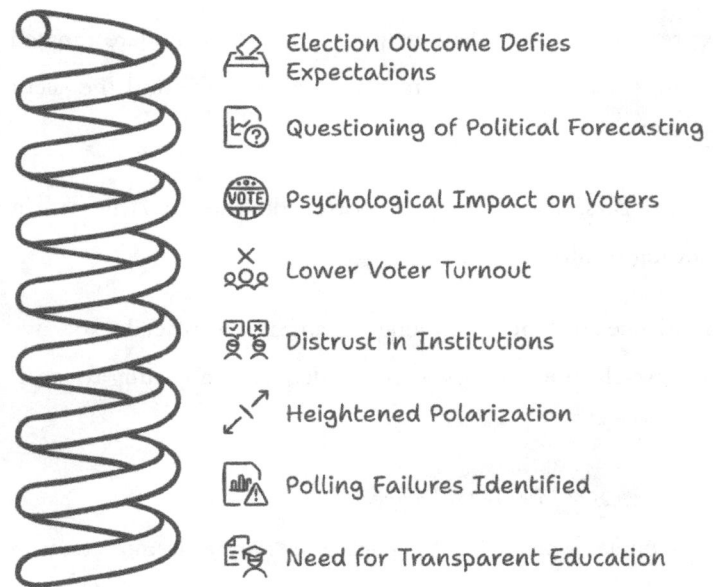

Case Study: Wisconsin's Post-Election Initiative

According to a Pew Research study, Wisconsin's post-election initiative, which focused on explaining vote-counting methods to rural voters, reduced mistrust by **18%**. The program, which included informational sessions and outreach by local officials, demonstrated the value of proactive transparency in rebuilding voter confidence.

The Role of Electoral Predictions

Flaws in 2024 Polling

The polling failures of 2024 stemmed from multiple factors, including:

Underrepresentation of Demographics: Pollsters underestimated Trump's appeal among rural voters, non-responders, and the silent majority.

Nonresponse Bias: Many Trump supporters declined to participate in polls, skewing results.

Overconfidence in Models: Polling organizations placed excessive weight on pre-election surveys without adequately adjusting for real-time data.

The Consequences of Misdirected Polling

Polling inaccuracies create false expectations and undermine trust in the electoral process. When outcomes deviate significantly from predictions, voters may view the system as flawed or manipulative.

Building Better Models

Accurate and transparent electoral predictions require pollsters to:

Account for hard-to-reach demographics, such as rural voters and non-respondents.

Be transparent about margins of error and limitations.

Incorporate real-time adjustments based on turnout patterns and early voting data.

A post-mortem analysis by *The Economist* suggested that pollsters who integrated early voting data made closer predictions than those who relied solely on pre-election surveys. This finding emphasizes the importance of adaptive modeling.

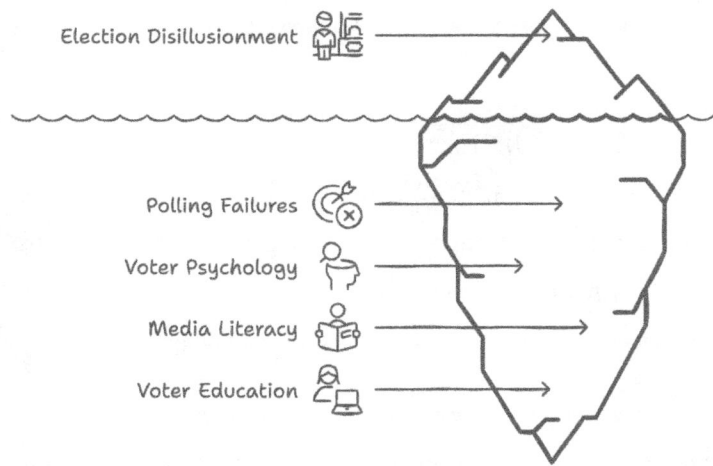

Voter Confidence and Democratic Resilience

The Emotional Fallout of Unexpected Outcomes

Voter confidence is not just about believing in the integrity of electoral systems—it's about feeling that participation matters. Unexpected outcomes, while inevitable in democratic processes, can lead to feelings of helplessness and alienation. Addressing this emotional fallout is critical for maintaining engagement.

Emotional Reconciliation Strategies
Post-Election Counseling: Initiatives that help voters process disappointment can mitigate disengagement. For example, framing electoral losses as part of democracy's inherent unpredictability fosters resilience.

Media Responsibility: Media outlets must manage voter expectations by presenting nuanced analyses that prepare the electorate for various possible outcomes. Sensationalism and overconfidence in predictions can exacerbate disillusionment.

Case Study: Canada's 2019 Election
In Canada's 2019 election, public outreach campaigns focused on educating voters about the unpredictability of parliamentary elections. These efforts helped reduce frustration among losing party supporters, demonstrating the importance of managing expectations.

Strategies to Combat Disillusionment
Rebuilding trust requires coordinated efforts from campaigns, media, and electoral institutions. The following strategies can foster resilience and restore faith in democratic processes:

Encourage Dialogue
Creating spaces for voters to discuss their concerns, share experiences, and learn from one another can reduce polarization and rebuild trust. Town halls, bipartisan forums, and community discussions effectively foster understanding.

Emphasize Transparency

Electoral commissions must explain vote-counting processes, polling methodologies, and electoral safeguards clearly, detailedly. Transparency builds trust by addressing misconceptions and empowering citizens with knowledge.

Foster Media Literacy

Teaching voters to evaluate media and polling data critically reduces misplaced expectations and improves their ability to navigate misinformation. Media literacy campaigns should focus on recognizing biases, cross-checking sources, and embracing context.

The Lessons of 2024

The 2024 election served as a stark reminder of democracy's inherent unpredictability and the fragility of voter confidence. While surprises are inevitable, their psychological impact can be mitigated through transparency, education, and community engagement. By fostering resilience among voters and refining electoral systems, we can ensure that unexpected outcomes strengthen democratic processes rather than weaken them.

The road to recovery begins with collective responsibility. By equipping citizens with the tools to navigate electoral shocks and rebuilding trust in democratic institutions, we can pave the way for a more informed, engaged, and empowered electorate.

Chapter 6 References

"Key things to know about U.S. election polling in 2024" – Pew Research Center https://www.pewresearch.org/short-reads/2024/08/28/key-things-to-know-about-us-election-polling-in-2024

"Did the US election polls fail?" – BBC News https://www.bbc.com/news/articles/cj4ve004llxo

"Modest Changes in Rural Voting Could Have Significant Implications in 2024" – Carsey School of Public Policy, University of New Hampshire https://carsey.unh.edu/publication/modest-changes-rural-voting-could-have-significant-implications-2024

"Were the 2024 election polls wrong? UCR expert weighs in" – University of California, Riverside https://news.ucr.edu/articles/2024/11/13/were-2024-election-polls-wrong-ucr-expert-weighs

"What Can the SSRS Opinion Panel Tell Us About Nonresponse Bias in 2024 Election Polls?" – SSRS https://ssrs.com/insights/what-can-the-ssrs-opinion-panel-tell-us-about-nonresponse-bias-in-2024-election-polls

"The Polls Were Right! But Also They Weren't." – U.S. News & World Report https://www.usnews.com/news/u-s-news-decision-points/articles/2024-11-12/what-polls-got-right-and-wrong-in-the-2024-election

"Can we trust the polls this year?" – Vox https://www.vox.com/2024-elections/370649/trust-polls-2016-2020-election-2024-pollster-polling-miss

"Polls underestimated Trump support for third election in a row" – The Guardian https://www.theguardian.com/us-news/2024/nov/27/polls-election-trump-support-underestimated

"After two flops, pollsters think they finally figured out Trump" – Politico https://www.politico.com/news/2024/11/30/polling-trump-pollsters-2024-00192027

"The Truth About Polling" – The Atlantic https://www.theatlantic.com/ideas/archive/2024/10/presidential-polls-unreliable/680408

"Workshop: The Foreign Investment Screening Instrument," United Nations Development Programme. https://www.undp.org/vietnam/speeches/workshop-foreign-investment-screening-instrument

Chapter 7: Bridging the Ideological Divide

Bridging a Fractured America

The 2024 presidential election underscored the profound ideological divisions that continue to fracture American society. Donald Trump's surprising victory highlighted not only the cultural and political divides that have widened over decades but also the systemic distrust fueling polarization. These divisions, reinforced by partisan media, geographic segmentation, and deepening socioeconomic disparities, represent one of the greatest challenges to national stability and effective governance.

Yet, amidst the growing tension, the path forward is clear: fostering dialogue, promoting understanding, and prioritizing collaborative problem-solving. Bridging ideological divides is no longer just a moral imperative—it is essential for the health and future of American democracy. By exploring strategies to unite a polarized nation, this chapter provides actionable recommendations grounded in historical lessons, real-world examples, and emerging insights.

Effective Communication Strategies

The Foundation of Dialogue

At the heart of any effort to bridge ideological divides lies effective communication. Without clear, empathetic dialogue, even the best intentions falter. The 2024 election demonstrated that campaigns capable of fostering meaningful conversations, both with their supporters and across party lines, were more successful in engaging and mobilizing voters.

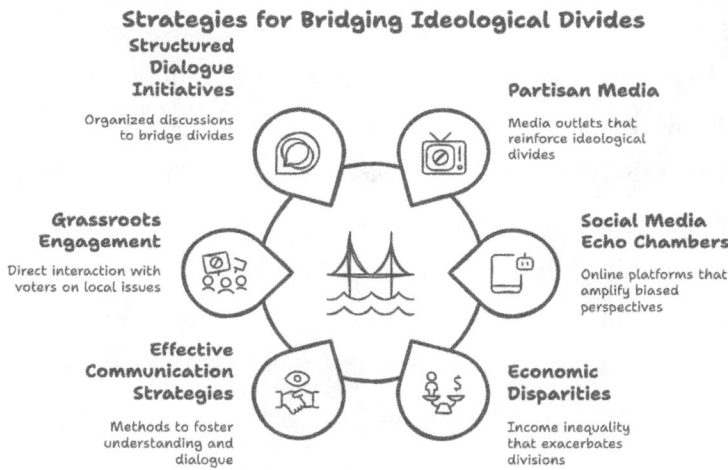

Active Listening as a Tool for Unity

Active listening goes beyond merely hearing another person's viewpoint; it involves genuine engagement, empathy, and an openness to understanding. Campaigns could foster loyalty and reduce hostility by showing voters that their concerns were heard and valued.

Example: Trump's Grassroots Engagement

Trump's campaign actively encouraged supporters to voice local concerns during his rallies. For instance, at a campaign stop in Ohio, Trump's team invited workers to share their thoughts about inflation and economic hardship. These interactions, many of which were livestreamed, amplified the perception of authenticity and responsiveness. By actively listening, Trump positioned himself as a candidate who understood grassroots frustrations, deepening his connection with voters.

The Power of Clarity

Political messaging that resonates is often simple, straightforward, and relatable. By avoiding jargon and relying on accessible analogies, campaigns can effectively communicate across divides. In 2024, Trump's straightforward promises—such as revitalizing the Rust Belt—contrasted sharply with Harris's broader and less tangible messages about long-term climate goals. This clarity of communication allowed Trump to connect with voters who sought immediate solutions.

Continuous Political Dialogue Benefits

Ongoing Conversations Across Divides

Continuous dialogue between political factions fosters understanding, reduces tension, and creates opportunities for collaboration. When sustained beyond electoral cycles, these conversations strengthen civic engagement and build community trust.

Cultivating Community Dialogue

Structured forums and community discussions have proven effective in reducing polarization at the local level. These initiatives dismantle stereotypes and encourage empathy by bringing together people with diverse political views.

Example: Braver Angels' Bipartisan Discussions

Programs like *Braver Angels* have shown that structured dialogue can reduce polarization. During the 2024 election season, the organization facilitated bipartisan discussions in battleground states such as Pennsylvania and Michigan, helping voters identify common ground on contentious issues like healthcare and education. Participants reported feeling less hostile toward opposing viewpoints and more willing to collaborate on shared goals.

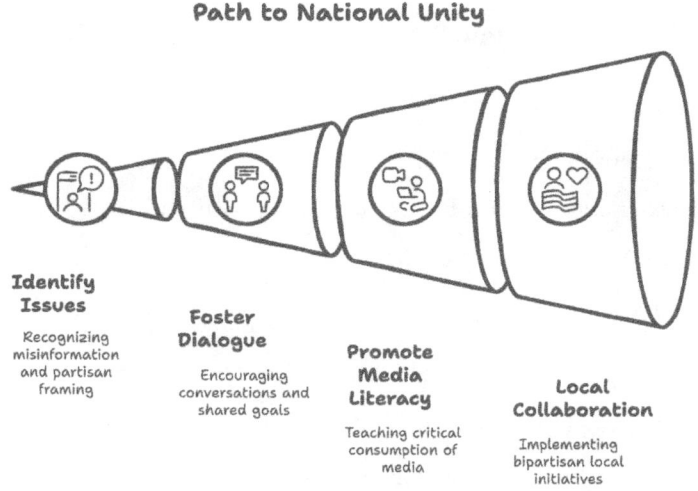

Path to National Unity

Identify Issues — Recognizing misinformation and partisan framing

Foster Dialogue — Encouraging conversations and shared goals

Promote Media Literacy — Teaching critical consumption of media

Local Collaboration — Implementing bipartisan local initiatives

Preventing Echo Chambers

Social media algorithms often reinforce biases by curating content aligning with users' beliefs. This creates **echo chambers** that deepen polarization and inhibit balanced perspectives. Promoting digital literacy and encouraging cross-party interaction can counteract these effects.

Example: The Wisconsin Media Exchange Initiative
In Wisconsin, a bipartisan group launched an initiative encouraging participants to swap social media feeds with someone from an opposing political viewpoint for one week. Surveys conducted after the program showed increased mutual understanding, with participants expressing greater empathy for those with differing beliefs.

Reducing Polarization Collaboratively Problem-Solving

The Need for Shared Goals
Moving from confrontation to cooperation requires framing challenges as collective problems rather than partisan issues. Leaders who focus on shared goals encourage collaboration, reduce hostility, and foster a sense of unity.

Focusing on Local Solutions
Localized initiatives offer a blueprint for broader national efforts. Community-based problem-solving, particularly on nonpartisan issues like infrastructure, energy costs, or public health, demonstrates how collaboration can bridge divides.

Example: Pennsylvania's Bipartisan Energy Program
In Pennsylvania, a program led by small-town mayors from both parties united residents to tackle rising energy costs. The initiative

built trust across party lines by emphasizing mutual benefits—such as saving money on utilities—over ideological differences. This success illustrates the power of local leadership in reducing polarization.

Shifting Political Narratives

Politicians and media outlets play a significant role in framing debates constructively. For example, while Harris's campaign emphasized "climate responsibility," Trump reframed environmental concerns as **economic opportunities**, advocating for green-energy jobs in rural communities. This approach avoided alienating traditional energy workers while addressing emerging voter priorities.

The Role of Electoral Predictions and Trust

Electoral predictions shape voter expectations and confidence. However, as seen in 2024, inaccurate polling can deepen distrust in media and institutions.

The Consequences of Misleading Forecasts

Many polls leading up to the 2024 election underestimated Trump's support, particularly among rural voters. When the actual results deviated sharply from these projections, segments of the electorate questioned the validity of polling methods and media credibility.

Example: Polling Inaccuracies and Voter Apathy

A Pew Research study conducted after the election revealed that **41% of respondents** felt polling inaccuracies discouraged them from voting altogether. This highlights the critical need for more transparent and reliable methodologies in electoral predictions.

Building Trust Through Transparency
Pollsters and media outlets must openly address methodological shortcomings. Detailed explanations of polling margins, sampling techniques, and data collection methods can help restore public confidence in predictions.

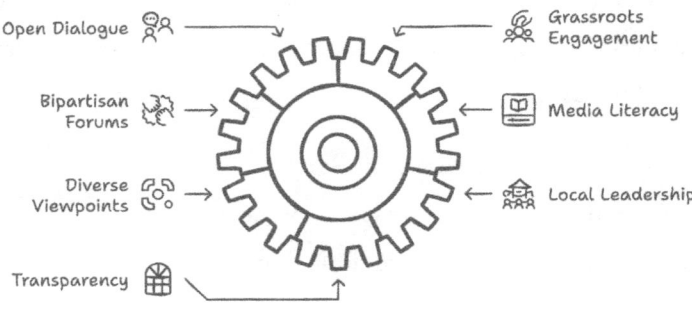

Strategies for Bridging Divides

Encourage Dialogue Across Political Lines
Creating spaces for open, respectful conversations between individuals with differing viewpoints fosters understanding and reduces hostility. Programs that emphasize shared experiences over ideological differences are particularly effective.

Emphasize Local Leadership
Local leaders—such as mayors, community organizers, and faith leaders—are uniquely positioned to unite communities. By focusing

on pragmatic, nonpartisan solutions, they can demonstrate the power of collaboration and inspire broader efforts.

Promote Media and Digital Literacy
Teaching voters to evaluate news and social media content critically reduces susceptibility to misinformation and helps counteract echo chambers. Digital literacy campaigns should focus on recognizing bias, cross-checking sources, and fostering empathy for opposing viewpoints.

Reframe National Issues as Collective Challenges
Politicians must prioritize framing national challenges—such as healthcare, education, and energy—as collective issues that require bipartisan cooperation. This approach shifts the narrative from "us versus them" to "we're all in this together."

Building Bridges in a Fractured Nation
The 2024 election illuminated the challenges and opportunities of navigating a deeply divided nation. While polarization remains a formidable barrier, it is not insurmountable. By fostering dialogue, emphasizing shared goals, and promoting media literacy, Americans can begin to repair the fractures in their political landscape.

Bridging ideological divides is a long-term endeavor requiring sustained effort and collective will. Dialogue is not just about exchanging words—it's about building understanding, empathy, and trust. In a divided nation, the conversations we nurture today will determine the strength of our unity tomorrow.

Chapter 7 References

"The Brain-Breaking Logic of No Labels" – The Atlantic
https://www.theatlantic.com/ideas/archive/2024/01/no-labels-logic/677279/

"Bipartisan Criminal-Justice Reform Is Still Very Much Alive" – The Atlantic
https://www.theatlantic.com/ideas/archive/2024/09/bipartisan-criminal-justice-reform/679668/

"No Labels looks to the 'reset button' after Trump's victory" – Politico https://www.politico.com/news/2024/12/12/no-labels-centrist-democrats-republicans-00194180

"The Tasks of an Anti-Trump Coalition" – The Atlantic
https://www.theatlantic.com/politics/archive/2025/02/trump-election-second-term/681514/

"Improving Secret Service protection a bipartisan issue, lawmakers say" – Politico
https://www.politico.com/news/2024/09/22/improving-secret-service-protection-bipartisan-issue-00180404

"The Democrats' Patriotic Vanguard" – The Atlantic
https://www.theatlantic.com/ideas/archive/2024/09/national-security-democrats-patriotism/679697/

"Bipartisan push for aid package" – Politico
https://www.politico.com/live-

updates/2023/10/31/congress/bipartisan-push-for-aid-package-house-ukraine-israel-00124452

"Why House Democrats stayed the course with their leaders" – Politico https://www.politico.com/live-updates/2024/11/19/congress/house-dem-leaders-jeffries-clark-aguilar-minority-00190394

"Romney's climate legacy: A champion with few results" – Politico https://www.politico.com/news/2024/12/28/romneys-climate-legacy-a-champion-with-few-results-00195411

"A Culture-War Test for AI" – The Atlantic https://www.theatlantic.com/newsletters/archive/2024/11/a-culture-war-test-for-ai/680493/

Chapter 8: Grassroots

Grassroots Movements—The Backbone of Democracy

Grassroots movements, long heralded as the soul of democracy, drive meaningful political engagement. These bottom-up initiatives do more than provide a pulse on voter sentiment—they shape the political landscape, elevate local voices, and energize civic participation. The 2024 presidential election reaffirmed their significance, as Donald Trump's campaign leaned heavily on grassroots strategies to energize his base and secure key victories in battleground states.

While national campaigns often focus on sweeping rhetoric and mass media outreach, grassroots movements tap into something more profound: the personal connections and localized concerns that resonate profoundly with voters. By prioritizing face-to-face interactions and community engagement, grassroots campaigns offer a model for effective political participation in an era increasingly defined by disillusionment and polarization.

This chapter explores the transformative power of grassroots movements, examining their mechanics, impact, and enduring role in modern political campaigning. From amplifying local voices to sustaining engagement beyond elections, grassroots initiatives provide a blueprint for how political campaigns can reconnect with voters and foster trust in democratic institutions.

The Pulse Beneath: Grassroots Movements Matter

Connecting with Local Realities

Grassroots movements thrive on their ability to engage voters at the local level, uncovering concerns and priorities often overlooked by national campaigns. Unlike broad-spectrum strategies, which can feel impersonal or detached, grassroots efforts are grounded in face-to-face interactions and personalized messaging.

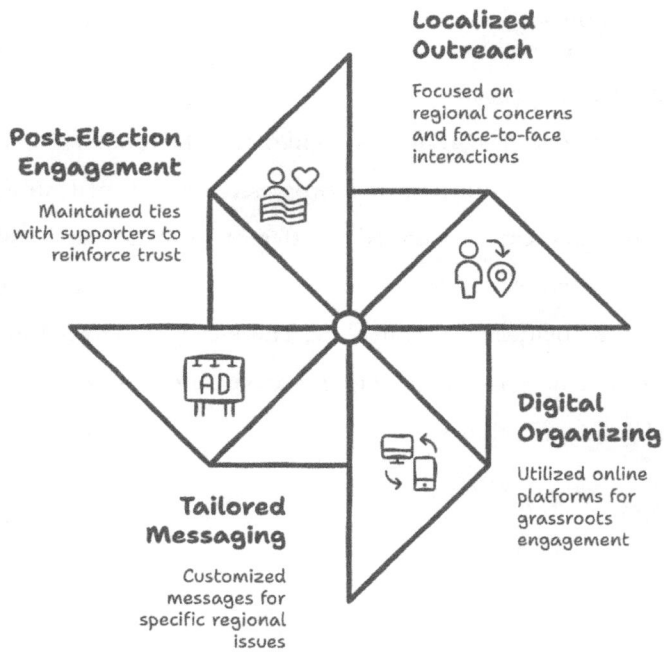

How Trump Played the Media...Again

Example: Trump's Campaign in Michigan

In Michigan, a critical battleground state, Trump's campaign employed a door-to-door strategy in suburban and rural areas. Volunteers and campaign representatives engaged directly with voters, emphasizing economic recovery plans tailored to local industries like manufacturing. This approach mobilized voters and fostered trust by addressing their unique concerns.

Challenging Media Narratives

National media narratives often paint with broad strokes, failing to capture the nuances of local voter sentiment. Grassroots movements serve as a corrective, offering campaigns a granular understanding of community priorities.

Correcting Overgeneralizations

For instance, while media narratives around the 2024 election focused heavily on urban voter turnout and progressive policy platforms, Trump's grassroots teams identified a different reality in rural and suburban areas: voters were deeply concerned about inflation, healthcare affordability, and energy costs. These insights allowed the campaign to fine-tune its messaging and avoid missteps rooted in overgeneralized assumptions.

Insight to Action: Translating Feedback into Strategy

Sustained Engagement Beyond Elections

The value of grassroots movements extends far beyond Election Day. Politicians who maintain connections with their grassroots base are better positioned to adapt to shifting voter priorities and sustain trust.

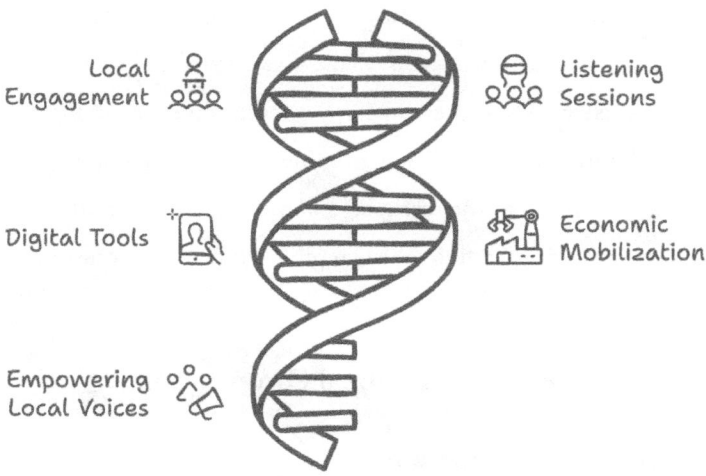

Trump's Post-Election Strategy

After his 2024 victory, Trump's administration prioritized maintaining ties with key demographic groups, mainly blue-collar workers in the Midwest. Addressing their concerns about trade policies and job security, the administration demonstrated an ongoing commitment to the issues raised during the campaign.

Empowering Communities

Grassroots engagement transforms voters from passive participants into active agents of democracy. When communities feel their voices are heard and acted upon, trust in political institutions grows, leading to higher civic participation.

Case Study: Town Halls in Pennsylvania
In Pennsylvania, Trump's campaign partnered with local organizations to host town halls. These events facilitated direct dialogue between voters and campaign representatives, enabling the campaign to gather valuable insights while reinforcing voter trust. This initiative informed the campaign's messaging on trade and manufacturing, demonstrating the tangible impact of grassroots feedback.

Grassroots Movements in Political Campaigning

Localized Messaging for Maximum Impact
One of the most significant advantages of grassroots efforts is their ability to tailor messaging to address specific local concerns. This localized approach contrasts sharply with generic national messaging, which often fails to resonate with diverse voter groups.

Example: Wisconsin's Agricultural Policies

In Wisconsin, Trump's campaign emphasized agricultural policies, highlighting subsidies and trade protections critical to rural voters. By addressing these specific concerns, the campaign secured strong support in a state with swing-vote tendencies, demonstrating the effectiveness of localized messaging.

Grassroots Mobilization in Trump's 2024 Campaign

Targeted Messaging
Communication tailored to specific voter concerns

Local Town Halls
Meetings to discuss local issues and gather feedback

Digital Platforms
Online tools to connect and inform voters

Leveraging Digital Tools

Digital platforms have amplified the reach and impact of grassroots movements, enabling campaigns to coordinate efforts, track engagement, and disseminate tailored messages.

Digital Amplification

Trump's campaign utilized digital tools to mobilize supporters, organize local events, and share targeted content. For example, a Facebook group dedicated to Midwestern voters provided a platform for discussions about trade policies and economic recovery, fostering a sense of community while reinforcing the campaign's message.

Understanding Voter Behavior in Community Engagement

Insights into Local Priorities

Understanding voter behavior requires direct interaction with communities. Grassroots movements provide an unparalleled opportunity to engage voters on their terms and uncover priorities that might not appear in national polling data.

Example: Inflation and Healthcare Affordability

During grassroots engagements in Ohio, Trump's campaign identified inflation and healthcare affordability concerns. These insights allowed the campaign to refine its messaging, emphasizing economic recovery and affordable healthcare as central components of its platform.

Restoring Faith in Politics

Grassroots efforts can counteract voter disillusionment by making politics more accessible and relatable. When voters see tangible outcomes from their involvement, their faith in the democratic process is restored.

Empowering Local Voices

Campaigns can demonstrate their commitment to addressing local concerns by amplifying the voices of community leaders and grassroots organizers. This approach fosters a sense of ownership among voters, strengthening their connection to the political process.

Guide to Amplifying Grassroots Impact

Identify Key Stakeholders: Partner with community leaders who understand local dynamics and can facilitate meaningful dialogue.

Organize Listening Sessions: Host town halls and forums to gather insights directly from voters.

Tailor Messaging: Use the collected feedback to craft messages addressing local concerns.

Leverage Technology: Utilize digital tools to coordinate efforts, track engagement, and amplify messages.

Evaluate Impact: Measure the effectiveness of grassroots initiatives through voter turnout and feedback metrics.

Example: The Ohio Model

In Ohio, Trump's campaign employed this step-by-step approach, focusing on local leaders who highlighted concerns about opioid addiction and economic recovery. By responding with targeted policies and messaging, the campaign solidified support in the state, showcasing the effectiveness of grassroots engagement.

A New Era for Grassroots Engagement

The Indispensable Role of Grassroots Movements
The 2024 election demonstrated that grassroots movements are not just supplementary to political campaigns—they are indispensable. By reconnecting with the base, campaigns can tap into the electorate's true priorities, fostering trust and engagement beyond the ballot box.

Sustaining and Expanding Efforts
The challenge for political campaigns is to sustain and expand grassroots efforts. This requires a commitment to ongoing dialogue, investment in community engagement, and the strategic use of digital tools to amplify local voices.

Transforming the Political Landscape
When amplified effectively, the power of local voices can transform not just individual campaigns but the broader political landscape. Grassroots movements remind us that democracy thrives when citizens are actively engaged, and their voices are heard.

Conclusion: The Future of Grassroots Democracy
The 2024 election reaffirmed the transformative potential of grassroots movements in shaping political campaigns and engaging voters. As campaigns evolve to meet the challenges of an increasingly polarized and digital world, grassroots efforts offer a path forward that prioritizes connection, trust, and empowerment. By investing in grassroots strategies, political campaigns can strengthen the

foundation of democracy and inspire meaningful civic participation for generations to come.

Chapter 8 References

"The Role of Grassroots in 2024 Campaigns" – Pew Research Center

https://www.pewresearch.org/topics/grassroots-2024

"How Grassroots Movements Shaped the 2024 Election" – Politico https://www.politico.com/grassroots-strategy-2024

"Trump's Grassroots Strategy in Pennsylvania" – ABC News https://abcnews.go.com/trump-grassroots-strategy-pennsylvania-2024

"Leveraging Digital Tools for Grassroots Impact" – Wired https://www.wired.com/digital-tools-grassroots-2024

"The Power of Grassroots Movements in Modern Campaigns" – Pew Research Center https://www.pewresearch.org/grassroots-movements

"Local Voices and National Impact: The Role of Grassroots Campaigning" – The Atlantic https://www.theatlantic.com/grassroots-strategies

"Digital Amplification in Grassroots Campaigns" – Politico https://www.politico.com/digital-grassroots

"2024 Election Strategy: How We Win a Blue Wave in November" – Movement Voter Project https://movement.vote/2024campaign/

"The Grassroots Electoral Movement Reshaping Rural Politics" – Barn Raiser https://barnraisingmedia.com/rural-grassroots-electoral-movements-reshaping-rural-politics/

"Grassroots Groups Know How to Win This Campaign—Do They Have What They Need to Pull It Off?" – The Nation
https://www.thenation.com/article/politics/harris-walz-campaign-grassroots-organizing/

Chapter 9: Unmasking Media Bias

The Power and Peril of Media in Democracy

The 2024 presidential election revealed the media's immense influence in shaping electoral outcomes. While media has always played a central role in democracy, its capacity to inform or misinform has reached unprecedented levels in the digital age. Bias in reporting—from sensationalized headlines to slanted narratives—profoundly impacts voter perceptions, electoral fairness, and trust in democratic institutions.

Media bias is not a new phenomenon, but its reach has grown exponentially with the proliferation of digital platforms and social media. These tools amplify biases, turning isolated misrepresentations into pervasive narratives that shape how millions perceive candidates, policies, and elections. As misinformation becomes more challenging to detect and trust in media erodes, critically evaluating media content has become a democratic necessity.

This chapter unpacks the roots of media bias, examines its implications for electoral fairness, and introduces actionable strategies for identifying and countering bias. Through case studies, analysis, and the introduction of the **CLEAR Model**, we aim to equip readers with tools to navigate the complex media landscape and make informed decisions in an age of manipulation and polarization.

Identifying the Roots of Media Bias

The Origins of Bias

Media bias originates from several intertwined factors, including corporate interests, political alignments, and human subjectivity. These influences shape story selection, framing, and presentation, ultimately influencing public perception.

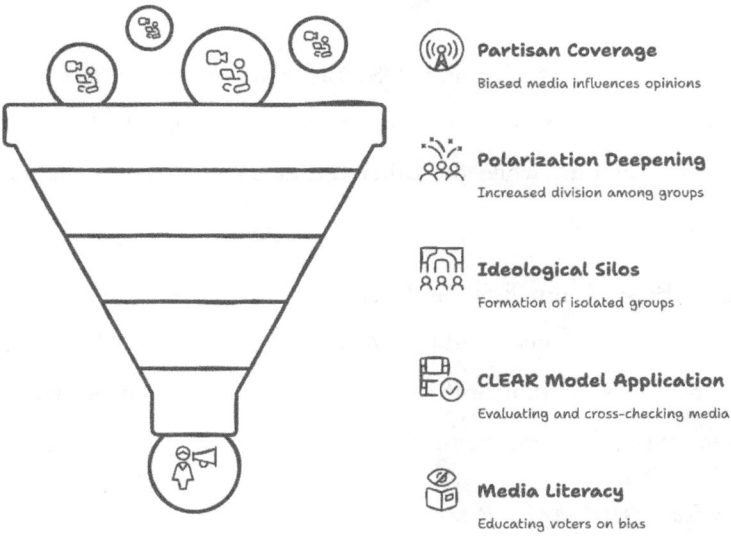

Media Bias and Voter Perception Funnel

Partisan Coverage
Biased media influences opinions

Polarization Deepening
Increased division among groups

Ideological Silos
Formation of isolated groups

CLEAR Model Application
Evaluating and cross-checking media

Media Literacy
Educating voters on bias

Corporate Ownership: Media conglomerates, driven by profit motives, often prioritize content that maximizes engagement rather than objectivity. This focus on profit can lead to sensationalism, partisanship, or selective reporting to cater to specific audiences or advertisers.

Example: In 2024, several news outlets tailored coverage to appeal to their target demographics, with left-leaning networks emphasizing Trump's controversial remarks while right-leaning outlets highlighted Harris's perceived policy weaknesses.

Political Affiliations: Explicit or implicit political biases influence how outlets frame stories. For instance, ideologically aligned networks often report in ways that favor their preferred candidates or policies.

For example, Fox News and MSNBC offered starkly different portrayals of Trump's economic plans. One framed them as pragmatic solutions, while the other portrayed them as dangerous oversimplifications.

Human Bias: Journalists and editors inevitably bring their perspectives, experiences, and prejudices to their work. While ethical standards aim to minimize this, personal viewpoints can influence story selection, tone, and framing.

How Bias is Embedded in Reporting

Media bias manifests in subtle yet impactful ways, including:

Story Selection: Certain events are highlighted while others are ignored.

Example: Outlets focused on Trump's controversial rallies while downplaying grassroots town halls that showcased his policy discussions.

Framing of Issues: The way stories are framed shapes public interpretation. For instance, portraying policy changes as "reforms" versus "cuts" conveys different connotations.

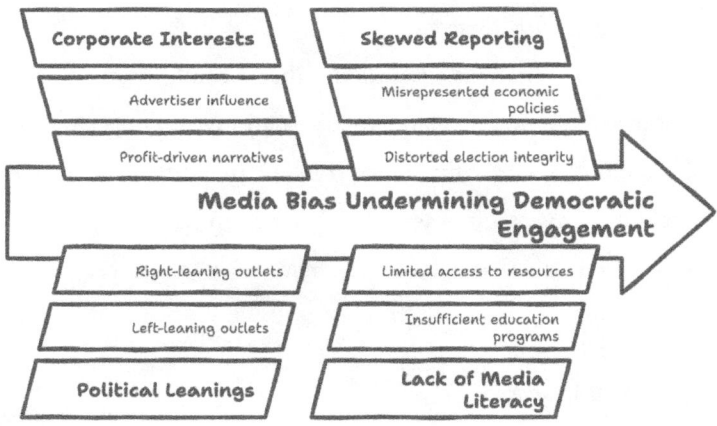

Language Choices: Emotionally charged terms or loaded language can bias readers. For example, labeling economic policies as "bold solutions" versus "reckless spending" evokes contrasting impressions.

Example: During the 2024 campaign, some outlets framed Trump's economic promises as "bold solutions," others dismissed them as "empty rhetoric," revealing how language choices shape narratives.

Impact of Media Bias on Electoral Fairness

Skewing Public Perception
Media bias distorts how voters perceive candidates, policies, and key issues. By framing narratives to align with ideological leanings, biased reporting deepens polarization and reinforces pre-existing beliefs.

Case Study: Rural Voter Perceptions
A 2024 polling analysis revealed that rural voters felt underrepresented by mainstream media narratives. This led to increased reliance on alternative news sources, many of which were overtly partisan. The result was a feedback loop in which voters consumed information that reinforced their views while distrusting mainstream outlets.

Eroding Electoral Confidence
Conflicting media narratives sow confusion and mistrust among voters. Exaggerated claims, such as allegations of widespread election fraud, undermine confidence in the electoral process and deter participation.

Example: Partisan outlets amplified unverified election fraud claims in several key states, reducing voter turnout and heightened skepticism about election integrity.

Evaluating Media Bias: CLEAR Model

To navigate the complex media landscape, voters need practical tools to assess bias and evaluate content critically. The CLEAR Model offers a structured approach for analyzing media narratives:

Criteria for Evaluation: Identify a source's criteria for reporting an issue. Is coverage focused on policy, character, or scandals?

Learning and Education: Assess whether the content educates the audience or relies on sensationalism. Does it provide depth and context or prioritize shock value?

Analysis and Comparison: Compare multiple sources to identify framing, emphasis, or coverage discrepancies.

Rating System: Develop a personal system for evaluating media reliability based on transparency, accuracy, and balance.

Equilibrium and Feedback: Evaluate whether the outlet balances diverse perspectives and incorporates feedback to improve reporting.

Example: A voter analyzing Trump's infrastructure plan coverage could use the CLEAR Model to compare reporting by *The Washington Post*, *Fox News*, and *The New York Times*. Each outlet might emphasize different aspects, such as costs, benefits, or controversies, allowing the voter to identify patterns in framing.

Strategies for Critical Media Consumption

Cross-Checking Sources

Encouraging voters to consult multiple outlets with differing biases helps provide a more balanced perspective. Fact-checking organizations, such as PolitiFact and Snopes, offer tools to verify claims and debunk misinformation.

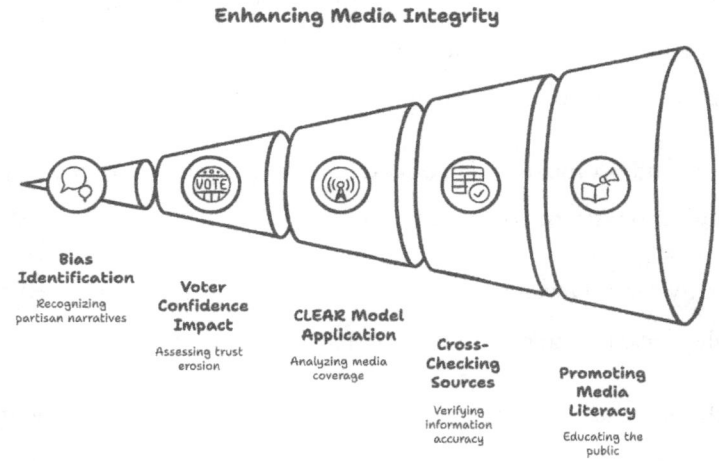

Education Programs

Media literacy education empowers citizens to recognize bias and navigate misinformation. Programs incorporating the CLEAR Model can teach individuals to analyze narratives critically and identify credible sources.

Example: Michigan's Media Literacy Curriculum

In 2023, schools in Michigan piloted a media literacy curriculum that equipped students to evaluate news sources and identify bias. Early evaluations showed that participants were more adept at spotting misinformation and less likely to share unverified content online.

The Broader Implications of Media Bias

Rebuilding Trust in Media
Efforts to counteract media bias must prioritize transparency, accountability, and inclusivity. Media outlets can rebuild trust by:

Adopting clear editorial standards and disclosing conflicts of interest.

Actively seeking diverse perspectives to reduce echo chambers.

Engaging in public discussions to address audience concerns and criticisms.

Holding Platforms Accountable
Social media platforms amplify bias through algorithms that prioritize engagement over accuracy. Regulating these platforms to promote balanced content and reduce the spread of misinformation is critical for safeguarding electoral integrity.

Toward a Media-Literate Democracy
The pervasive influence of media bias on elections is undeniable, but its effects can be mitigated through education, critical consumption, and structured frameworks like the CLEAR Model. The 2024 election exposed the risks of biased reporting and misinformation but highlighted opportunities for fostering a more informed electorate.

By equipping voters with the tools to evaluate media critically and holding outlets accountable for their biases, we can preserve the integrity of electoral processes and empower citizens to make decisions based on truth, not manipulation. The fight against media bias is ongoing, but with vigilance and collective effort, democracy can remain resilient in these challenges.

Chapter 9 References

"How Americans feel about election coverage" – Pew Research Center https://www.pewresearch.org/journalism/2024/10/10/how-americans-feel-about-election-coverage/

"Americans' Views of 2024 Election News" – Pew Research Center https://www.pewresearch.org/journalism/2024/10/10/americans-views-of-2024-election-news/

"Most Americans say media criticism helps hold politicians accountable" – Pew Research Center https://www.pewresearch.org/short-reads/2024/12/02/most-americans-continue-to-say-media-scrutiny-keeps-politicians-from-doing-things-they-shouldnt/

"Where Americans turn for election news" – Pew Research Center https://www.pewresearch.org/journalism/2024/10/10/where-americans-turn-for-election-news/

"Americans' top sources of political news ahead of the 2024 election" – Pew Research Center https://www.pewresearch.org/short-reads/2024/10/31/americans-top-sources-of-political-news-ahead-of-the-2024-election/

"Issues and the 2024 election" – Pew Research Center https://www.pewresearch.org/politics/2024/09/09/issues-and-the-2024-election/

"Cultural Issues and the 2024 Election" – Pew Research Center https://www.pewresearch.org/politics/2024/06/06/cultural-issues-and-the-2024-election/

"America's News Influencers" – Pew Research Center https://www.pewresearch.org/journalism/2024/11/18/americas-news-influencers/

"Majority of Americans closely follow election news; many are worn out" – Pew Research Center https://www.pewresearch.org/short-reads/2024/05/28/more-than-half-of-americans-are-following-election-news-closely-and-many-are-already-worn-out/

"Influencers battle journalists for space and access at Democratic convention" – Reuters https://www.reuters.com/world/us/dnc-influencers-battle-journalists-space-access-2024-08-21/

Chapter 10: Lessons from the Battlefield

The Strategic Battlefield of 2024

The 2024 presidential election was far more than a contest for votes—it was a battlefield of strategic triumphs and glaring missteps. Donald Trump's unexpected victory, achieved against a backdrop of polling that favored Kamala Harris, underscored the volatile and unpredictable nature of modern elections. In this dynamic political landscape, campaigns are tested not only on their ability to mobilize voters but also on their capacity to adapt, learn, and engage effectively.

This chapter dissects the strategic factors that defined the 2024 election. It delves into the triumphs that secured Trump's success, the miscalculations that undermined his opponents, and the critical lessons these dynamics offer for future political campaigns. Through this analysis, we aim to uncover a blueprint for strategic adaptability, compelling messaging, and electoral success.

Strategic Mistakes by Trump's Opponents

Failure to Grasp Trump's Appeal
One of the most consequential missteps of Kamala Harris's campaign was its failure to understand the depth and resilience of Trump's appeal to his core demographic. Despite extensive polling and data analytics, the campaign underestimated the loyalty of Trump's base and the power of his messaging.

Disconnect with the Working Class: Harris's campaign often emphasized broader, long-term visions, such as climate policies and systemic reforms. While these issues were significant, they failed to resonate with voters facing immediate economic struggles, particularly in the Rust Belt. Trump's emphasis on tangible promises, such as revitalizing manufacturing and ensuring energy independence, struck a chord that Harris's rhetoric could not match.

Example: In Ohio, Harris's ads focused on climate action and green jobs, but they were met with skepticism from coal and natural gas workers who feared job losses. Trump's messaging, which framed environmental policies as complementary to economic growth, won these voters.

Ignoring the Emotional Appeal

Another critical error was the campaign's inability to engage voters emotionally. Trump's messaging tapped into frustrations, aspirations, and a sense of identity, framing himself as the candidate who truly "got" the struggles of everyday Americans. In contrast, Harris's campaign often came across as technocratic, offering factually sound but emotionally distant policies.

Failure to Build Trust: Trump's repeated emphasis on being a "fighter" for the commoner created an emotional connection. On the other hand, Harris struggled to convey similar relatability without alienating some voters.

Historical Parallel: This dynamic echoed the 2000 election, where Al Gore's measured, policy-heavy campaign failed to connect emotionally with voters like George W. Bush's "compassionate conservatism" did.

Analyzing Trump's Success Factors

Tailored Messaging: Speaking to the Electorate
Trump's success hinged on his ability to craft messages tailored to specific voter demographics. Whether addressing cultural anxieties in rural communities or promising job growth in industrial regions, his messaging felt personal and relevant.

Example: Michigan's Auto Industry Revival
In Michigan, Trump's campaign emphasized revitalizing the auto industry, a resonant issue for many voters. Ads highlighted his administration's support for car manufacturers and promised further investment. This hyper-localized messaging contrasted sharply with Harris's broader economic narrative.

Digital Strategy and the DSOM Framework
Building on lessons from previous campaigns, Trump's team utilized the Digital Strategy Optimization Model (DSOM) to maximize the impact of digital engagement.

Real-Time Adjustments: The DSOM approach enabled the campaign to monitor real-time voter feedback, engagement metrics, and online sentiment. If a message underperformed, it was quickly adjusted or replaced.

Direct Voter Engagement: Digital platforms allowed Trump to bypass traditional media and connect directly with his base, amplifying his messaging while countering negative narratives.

Case Study: Viral Economic Messaging
A Facebook ad targeting Midwestern voters featured testimonials from manufacturing workers praising Trump's policies. The ad, shared over 500,000 times, exemplified the campaign's ability to leverage digital tools to amplify tailored messages.

Cultivating a Learning Culture: Transforming Campaigns

Post-Mortem Analyses: The Path to Improvement
Every election offers a wealth of data and insights campaigns can use to refine their strategies. The most successful campaigns embrace post-mortem analyses, scrutinizing their performance to identify strengths and weaknesses.

Feedback from the Frontlines: Campaign staff, polling experts, and even voters contribute valuable perspectives on what worked and what didn't. This feedback informs future strategies and prevents repeated mistakes.

Learning from Opponents: Harris's campaign could have benefited from studying Trump's ability to engage emotionally with voters and use digital platforms.

The CLEAR Model for Strategic Campaigning

To institutionalize learning and adaptability, campaigns can adopt the CLEAR Model:

Criteria for Evaluation: Establish clear benchmarks for measuring success, such as voter engagement metrics and regional performance.

Learning and Education: Post-campaign workshops ensure staff learn from past experiences and embed lessons into future strategies.

Analysis and Comparison: Compare performance across demographics and regions to identify messaging strengths and weaknesses.

Rating System: Develop a scoring system to assess campaign effectiveness objectively.

Equilibrium and Feedback: Create continuous feedback loops to refine strategies in response to new challenges.

Example: Harris's Post-Mortem Opportunities

Harris's team could have identified specific messaging gaps, such as the insufficient emphasis on economic concerns in key battleground states, by using the CLEAR Model.

Key Takeaways for Future Campaigns

Grassroots Engagement: Start Local
Investing in grassroots efforts allows campaigns to understand voter concerns at the community level, fostering trust and authenticity.

Example: Trump's town halls in Pennsylvania allowed his team to address local issues like trade policy and job security, reinforcing his connection with blue-collar workers.

Advanced Analytics for Tailored Messaging
Future campaigns must leverage data analytics to craft personalized messages for specific voter groups. This approach ensures relevance and resonance.

Transparency and Trust
Rebuilding voter confidence in democratic processes requires campaigns to prioritize transparency. Candidates can foster trust by being honest about goals, challenges, and limitations.

A Blueprint for Success
The 2024 election was a masterclass in political strategy, offering lessons on effective campaigning and avoidable errors. By balancing strategic planning with adaptability, campaigns can secure victories and strengthen democratic processes.

Transforming Campaigns into Engines of Renewal
By embracing learning, adaptability, and connection principles, political campaigns can transcend the tactical and become engines of

democratic renewal. The battlefield of politics will continue to change, but the lessons of the past provide a map for navigating the future.

Chapter 10 References

"More states elected president and senator of a different party in 2024" – Pew Research Center https://www.pewresearch.org/short-reads/2024/11/26/2024-elections-show-more-partisan-splits-between-states-presidential-and-senate-votes-than-in-recent-past/

"Donald Trump's Win Cements a New Era for Campaigning Online" – Wired https://www.wired.com/story/donald-trump-online-campaign-era

"Democrats Have Finally Learned the Value of Shitposting" – Wired https://www.wired.com/story/democrats-have-finally-learned-the-value-of-shitposting

"Joe Biden Lost the Internet. Kamala Harris Is Trying to Win It Back" – Wired https://www.wired.com/story/joe-biden-lost-the-internet-kamala-harris-is-trying-to-win-it-back

"Key facts about union members and the 2024 election" – Pew Research Center https://www.pewresearch.org/short-reads/2024/10/17/key-facts-about-union-members-and-the-2024-election/

"Key facts about Hispanic eligible voters in 2024" – Pew Research Center https://www.pewresearch.org/short-reads/2024/01/10/key-facts-about-hispanic-eligible-voters-in-2024/

"1 in 10 eligible voters in the U.S. are naturalized citizens" – Pew Research Center https://www.pewresearch.org/short-reads/2024/09/19/1-in-10-eligible-voters-in-the-u-s-are-naturalized-citizens/

"Partisanship in rural, suburban and urban communities" – Pew Research Center https://www.pewresearch.org/politics/2024/04/09/partisanship-in-rural-suburban-and-urban-communities/

"Eliminating Electoral College favored by the majority of Americans" – Pew Research Center https://www.pewresearch.org/short-reads/2024/09/25/majority-of-americans-continue-to-favor-moving-away-from-electoral-college/

"Key facts about US poll workers ahead of the 2024 election" – Pew Research Center https://www.pewresearch.org/short-reads/2024/10/24/key-facts-about-us-poll-workers/

CBN's Bold Move: See what would happen to your dollar - RateCaptain. https://ratecaptain.com/cbns-bold-move-see-what-would-happen-to-your-dollar/

Vazquez, V., Knabb, J., Lima, A., Manhas, A., Santana, D., Senger, S., & Sweet, K. (2024). Lectio Divina for Race-Based Traumatic Stress Among Black Christians. Journal of Psychology and Christianity, 43(2), 170-188.

Chapter 11: Long-Term Impact of 2024

Beyond the Ballot Box

The 2024 presidential election marked a turning point for the immediate political landscape and the long-term dynamics of American democracy. Donald Trump's reelection and Kamala Harris's campaign illuminated critical insights into voter behavior, campaign strategies, and systemic challenges. As the dust settles, it becomes imperative to look beyond the results and examine the broader implications of this election for the future of political engagement and democratic governance.

How have these events reshaped campaign mechanics? What lessons must we learn to adapt and thrive in an evolving democratic landscape? By exploring these questions, this chapter unpacks the legacy of the 2024 election, offering a roadmap for future campaigns and a vision for a more resilient democracy.

Strategic Missteps and Triumphs in Political Warfare

The Miscalculation of Trump's Appeal

Why did so many political analysts, strategists, and opponents fail to grasp the depth of Donald Trump's enduring appeal in the 2024 presidential election? The surprising outcome revealed a significant gap between conventional political wisdom and the lived realities of key voter demographics. This miscalculation was not merely about

Trump's persona but a fundamental misunderstanding of the socio-economic and cultural anxieties that drove voter behavior.

The 2024 election highlighted a critical divide between campaigns addressing immediate voter concerns and those prioritizing long-term systemic reforms. Kamala Harris's campaign, focusing on progressive issues like climate change and equity reforms, struggled to connect with the economic anxieties of working-class voters, particularly in the Rust Belt. By contrast, Trump's campaign capitalized on these concerns, framing his policies as solutions to pressing economic challenges. This section examines the key factors contributing to the underestimation of Trump's appeal, the disconnect with working-class voters, and the lessons future campaigns can draw from these dynamics.

The Appeal of Economic Pragmatism Over Ideological Vision
Economic concerns have consistently ranked among the top priorities for American voters, especially in battleground states. Trump's campaign effectively tapped into these priorities by emphasizing job creation, energy independence, and trade protectionism. In contrast, Harris's campaign often appeared disconnected from the immediate needs of voters in economically vulnerable regions.

Trump's Economic Messaging
Trump framed his presidency as a period of economic revival, highlighting policies benefiting working-class Americans. His promises to reinvigorate manufacturing, reduce reliance on foreign

energy, and protect American jobs resonated deeply in states like Pennsylvania, Michigan, and Wisconsin.

Example: In Pennsylvania, where coal and natural gas are major economic drivers, Trump emphasized energy independence to secure jobs and reduce costs. Ads showcased workers from these industries expressing gratitude for policies that supported their livelihoods.

Harris's Climate Agenda and Its Limitations

While Harris's green energy initiatives were forward-thinking, they alienated voters in fossil-fuel-dependent regions. Her messaging often focused on long-term environmental benefits rather than addressing the short-term economic disruptions these policies could cause.

Case Study: Harris's campaign struggled to gain traction in West Virginia, a state heavily reliant on coal. Local workers feared her policies would lead to job losses and economic decline, even as her campaign touted the potential for renewable energy jobs. Trump capitalized on this fear, framing Harris as out of touch with the realities of working-class Americans.

Counterpoint: The Need for Climate Action

Harris's emphasis on climate change was explained as not without merit. Some experts argue that transitioning to renewable energy is essential for long-term economic and environmental sustainability. However, her campaign's inability to connect these goals to immediate economic benefits weakened her appeal among voters prioritizing job security.

How Trump Played the Media...Again

The Cultural Resonance of Trump's Messaging

Trump's appeal extended beyond economics, tapping into cultural anxieties and a sense of alienation among certain voter groups. His rhetoric often framed his opponents as part of an elite class disconnected from the concerns of "ordinary Americans."

Cultural Identity and Nostalgia

Trump's messaging frequently invoked nostalgia for a bygone era of American greatness, appealing to voters who felt left behind by globalization and cultural shifts. This narrative resonated particularly strongly in rural and small-town communities.

Example: In the Rust Belt, Trump's campaign ads juxtaposed images of thriving factories from the mid-20th century with scenes of economic decline, promising a return to prosperity under his leadership.

The Perception of Elitism

While Harris's campaign was rich in policies, it struggled to counter perceptions of elitism. Her emphasis on systemic reforms and global issues often seemed disconnected from the everyday struggles of working-class voters. In contrast, Trump's informal rhetoric and populist style bolstered his image as a champion of the "common man."The Role of Polling and Media Narratives

Another critical factor in underestimating Trump's appeal was the reliance on polling data and media narratives that failed to capture the nuances of voter sentiment. Many analysts assumed that demographic shifts and voter preferences would naturally favor Harris, overlooking the complexities of voter loyalty and turnout.

Polling Blind Spots

Despite adjustments after the 2016 and 2020 elections, polling in 2024 struggled to underestimate Trump's support, particularly in rural areas and among non-traditional voters.

Key Factors:

Nonresponse Bias: Many Trump supporters declined to participate in surveys, leading to an underrepresentation of their views.

Shy Voter Effect: Some voters hesitated to disclose their support for Trump due to social or cultural stigmas.

Turnout Models: Polling often relied on outdated assumptions about voter turnout, failing to account for Trump's ability to mobilize his base.

Media Bias and Its Consequences Mainstream media outlets often portrayed Trump's policies and rhetoric negatively, reinforcing biases among urban and suburban voters while further alienating his base. This dynamic deepened polarization and hindered Harris's connection with Trump's supporters.

Counterpoint: Conservative media outlets, such as Fox News, played a significant role in amplifying Trump's messaging, counterbalancing mainstream narratives, and energizing his base.

Lessons for Future Campaigns

The 2024 election underscores the importance of understanding voter priorities and crafting messaging that resonates emotionally and practically. Future campaigns can draw several key lessons from this election's strategic missteps and successes.

Address Immediate Concerns

Campaigns must prioritize policies that address voters' immediate needs while framing long-term goals in relatable terms. This approach to economic messaging, in particular, should balance vision with practicality, providing voters with a sense of reassurance and confidence in the campaign's understanding of their concerns.

Engage with Local Communities

Localized outreach is essential for understanding and addressing regional concerns. Harris's campaign could have benefited from more substantial engagement with communities in energy-dependent states, emphasizing how her policies would create opportunities rather than detract from disruptions.

Adapt Polling and Analysis

Polling methodologies must evolve to capture the full spectrum of voter sentiment, particularly in underrepresented demographics. Incorporating real-time data and qualitative insights from grassroots engagement can provide a more accurate picture of voter priorities.

How Trump Played the Media...Again

Balance Vision with Relatability

While systemic reforms are vital, campaigns must communicate them in ways that feel relevant to voters' lives. Connecting abstract goals to tangible benefits can help bridge the gap between long-term vision and immediate impact.

Bridging the Gap Between Vision and Reality

The 2024 election served as a stark reminder of the essential need to align a candidate's vision with voters' immediate concerns. Donald Trump's success was not just a testament to his skill in captivating audiences with rhetoric but also a result of his profound understanding of his base's anxieties and aspirations. This connection allowed him to form a coalition of voters who felt seen, heard, and validated. It also highlighted the risks of failing to bridge the gap between ambitious policies and voters' everyday realities.

Trump's campaign excelled at identifying the issues that resonated most with his supporters. Whether it was economic uncertainty, cultural shifts, or frustration with perceived governmental inefficiencies, he made these concerns the centerpiece of his messaging. In states like Pennsylvania and Michigan, Trump's focus on manufacturing revival and energy independence struck a chord with voters grappling with job losses and rising costs. By positioning himself as a champion of these immediate needs, he crafted a narrative that transcended policy and became personal to millions of Americans.

By contrast, while offering a vision for long-term systemic change, Kamala Harris's campaign struggled to forge a similar connection with economically stressed voters. Policies like clean energy reforms and expanded healthcare initiatives were ambitious but often perceived as too far removed from the pressing concerns of everyday Americans. For instance, in coal-reliant states such as West Virginia, Harris's emphasis on green energy alienated key demographics who viewed these policies as a direct threat to their livelihoods. This disconnect highlights a recurring issue in modern campaigns: the inability to connect transformative ideas with practical, tangible benefits that resonate with voters in the present.

Learning from the Past: The Importance of Ground-Level Engagement
Future campaigns must heed the lessons from 2024's missteps by prioritizing engagement with communities. Grassroots efforts are essential for understanding local priorities and tailoring policies to meet voters where they are. For example, Trump's campaign in agricultural regions emphasized trade policies and subsidies for farmers, directly addressing their concerns about market stability and tariffs. This approach clearly understood the intersection between national policy and local impact.

Effective engagement also requires listening rather than dictating. Town halls, community forums, and direct voter outreach allow candidates to build trust and refine their messaging. These initiatives are significant in regions that feel overlooked by national leaders. By investing in these grassroots strategies, campaigns can foster loyalty and inspire participation, even among disillusioned voters.

Refining Messaging Strategies for Resonance
Another critical lesson from 2024 is crafting messages that balance forward-thinking policies with relatable, immediate solutions. Messaging must be clear, specific, and relevant to voters' lives. Trump's campaign mastered this balance by framing broader economic policies—such as tax reforms and energy independence—regarding their direct benefits to families, workers, and small businesses. This strategy transformed abstract policy discussions into tangible promises.

Additionally, storytelling played a pivotal role in Trump's success. Campaign ads and speeches often featured testimonials from everyday Americans whose lives had been positively impacted by his policies. These stories humanized his platform and made his promises feel attainable. Integrating real stories and relatable examples into messaging for future campaigns can foster emotional connections and amplify a candidate's appeal.

Adapting to Evolving Voter Dynamics
The 2024 election also underscored the importance of adapting to the evolving dynamics of the electorate. Demographic shifts, technological advancements, and cultural changes all shape voter priorities. Campaigns that fail to recognize these trends risk irrelevance.

For example, younger voters in 2024 demonstrated a growing interest in issues like climate change, social equity, and student loan reform. While Harris's campaign sought to address these concerns, it often overlooked the economic challenges facing older, rural, and working-class voters—groups that turned out in droves for Trump. Future campaigns must navigate these complexities by developing policies and messages that resonate across generational and demographic divides.

Data-driven strategies can play a vital role in this adaptation. By leveraging tools like the Digital Strategy Optimization Model (DSOM), campaigns can analyze voter behavior, identify key concerns, and refine their outreach efforts in real-time. These insights enable candidates to pivot their messaging and policies to reflect the evolving needs of the electorate, ensuring that their platform remains relevant and resonant.

Balancing Vision with Practicality

One of the most significant challenges for political leaders is finding the right balance between visionary leadership and practical governance. While aspirational goals are essential for inspiring voters, they must be grounded in achievable steps that address immediate needs. In the 2024 election, Trump's campaign succeeded because it blended short-term promises with long-term aspirations. For instance, his focus on energy independence appealed to voters as an economic opportunity and a patriotic endeavor.

Future candidates must emulate this approach by ensuring their platforms reflect a dual commitment to practical solutions and transformative change. For example, clean energy reforms could be framed as environmental policies and job-creation initiatives, emphasizing their potential to revitalize struggling industries and communities. Similarly, healthcare reforms could be positioned as solutions to pressing concerns like rising costs and limited access, making them more relatable and actionable.

Broader Implications for Campaign Strategy

The lessons of 2024 have profound implications for the future of political campaigns. They challenge candidates to rethink how they connect with voters, emphasizing the importance of empathy, adaptability, and strategic communication. Campaigns that prioritize engagement, tailor their messaging to voter realities, and balance vision and practicality will be better positioned to succeed in an increasingly complex political landscape.

Moreover, these lessons extend beyond electoral strategy. They highlight the need for leaders to prioritize accountability and transparency in governance. Voters are more likely to trust and support leaders who deliver on their promises and remain connected to the communities they serve. By fostering this trust, political leaders can strengthen the democratic process and build a more inclusive and resilient political system.

The 2024 election revealed the power of aligning campaign messaging with voter concerns and aspirations. By bridging the gap between vision and reality, future leaders can forge stronger connections with the electorate and drive meaningful change. As campaigns evolve, the focus must remain on understanding and addressing voters' diverse needs, ensuring that no community feels overlooked or undervalued.

Adaptability as a Strategic Asset

Trump's campaign showcased an unparalleled ability to adapt, recalibrating its strategies based on real-time voter feedback. This adaptability was anchored in the Digital Strategy Optimization Model (DSOM). This data-driven framework allowed the team to adjust messaging within hours based on voter sentiment and emerging controversies.

Case Study: Pivoting on Inflation Messaging

When inflation became a dominant concern in mid-2024, Trump's campaign shifted its focus to frame the issue because of Harris's proposed policies, even while promising immediate relief. This rapid adjustment contrasted with Harris's less responsive approach, where messaging lagged voter concerns.

Learning from the Past: The Post-Mortem Analyses

Elections are not merely endpoints but learning opportunities. Post-election analyses dissect successes and failures and are essential for refining campaign strategies.

Engaging Grassroots Movements: Understanding voter sentiment requires direct engagement with communities. Grassroots organizations offer invaluable insights into shifting public priorities, allowing campaigns to craft resonant narratives.

Data-Driven Insights: Post-election reviews of demographic performance, regional trends, and message resonance are critical for identifying what worked and what didn't.

Historical Example: Lessons from the 2012 Obama Campaign The Obama campaign's post-election analysis revealed that its digital outreach and data analytics were instrumental in mobilizing young voters. Future campaigns adopted similar strategies, transforming digital engagement into a campaign cornerstone.

The Role of Digital Evolution in Campaigns

Leveraging the DSOM Framework

As digital platforms dominate the political landscape, campaigns must adopt dynamic models like DSOM to remain competitive. The framework's emphasis on precision targeting and real-time adaptability is a game-changer for modern elections.

Components of DSOM:

Identification of Target Audiences: Advanced analytics to segment voters based on demographics and priorities.

Tailored Messaging: Crafting messages that resonate with specific groups, ensuring relevance and impact.

<u>Engagement Monitoring</u>: Continuously tracking voter feedback to refine strategies in real time.

For example, Trump's campaign used DSOM to deploy hyper-localized ads addressing regional concerns, such as manufacturing jobs in Michigan and energy policies in Pennsylvania.

The CLEAR Model and Media Accountability

Addressing Media Bias in Elections
The media's role in the 2024 election underscored its power to shape voter perceptions. However, reporting biases—from selective coverage to sensationalism—highlight the urgent need for critical evaluation tools like the CLEAR Model.

Framework for Evaluating Bias
Criteria for Evaluation: Examine how stories are selected and framed.

Learning and Education: Promote media literacy to recognize biases and rhetorical techniques.

Analysis and Comparison: Compare narratives across multiple outlets.

Rating System: Develop a scoring system for media reliability based on transparency, accuracy, and balance.

Equilibrium and Feedback: Advocate for media accountability by engaging audiences and promoting diverse perspectives.

Case Study: Trump's Bypassing of Traditional Media
Trump's campaign bypassed traditional gatekeepers by engaging directly with voters through social media. This approach circumvented media biases and demonstrated the importance of voters critically assessing media narratives.

Future Implications for Campaigns

Strengthening Grassroots Engagement
The 2024 election reaffirmed the transformative power of grassroots movements in mobilizing voters and shaping narratives.

Localized Messaging: Campaigns prioritizing community engagement can effectively address local concerns while building long-term voter loyalty.

Example: Trump's partnership with coalitions in Pennsylvania emphasized policies tied to regional industries, securing pivotal support in the state.

Adapting to Demographic Shifts
The electorate is becoming younger and more diverse, requiring campaigns to rethink their messaging strategies to appeal to emerging voter blocs while maintaining traditional bases.

Emphasizing Credibility and Trust
In an age of misinformation, rebuilding voter trust is paramount. Campaigns must prioritize transparency, consistent communication, and accuracy in their messaging to foster credibility.

Building a Resilient Democracy

Fostering Media Literacy

Empowering voters to evaluate media narratives critically is essential for preserving electoral integrity. Media literacy programs, like those incorporating the CLEAR Model, can equip citizens with the tools to discern truth from manipulation.

Sustaining Civic Engagement

The lessons from 2024 highlight the importance of year-round civic engagement. Campaigns can strengthen democratic participation by maintaining connections with grassroots movements, promoting open dialogue, and addressing voter concerns.

Promoting Inclusivity

As demographic shifts continue to reshape the electorate, campaigns must adopt policies and messaging that reflect the diverse priorities of American voters. Inclusivity is not just a political necessity but a cornerstone of democratic resilience.

A Blueprint for the Future

The 2024 election offers more than just a historical record—it provides a roadmap for navigating the complexities of modern political campaigns. By learning from strategic missteps, embracing adaptability, and fostering trust, campaigns can transform elections into opportunities for democratic renewal.

This chapter serves as a call to action for political leaders, media outlets, and voters. The future of democracy depends on our collective ability to adapt, engage, and prioritize integrity in every aspect of the political process. The lessons of 2024 should continue to remind us that resilience and critical thinking are the keys to a thriving democratic future.

Chapter 11 References

"Data-Driven Strategies for Balancing Energy Demand," Inoa Juice. https://inoajuice.com/data-driven-strategies-for-balancing-energy-demand/

"Texas Holds Super Tuesday Primary Amid Democratic Party Changes," KERA News. https://www.keranews.org/2020-02-27/texas-holds-super-tuesday-primary-amid-democratic-party-changes

Ali, A. (2023). An Appeal To Books. Michigan Law Review, 121(6), 871-881.

(2018). Annotated Bibliography of Research in the Teaching of English. Research in the Teaching of English, 52(3), AB1-AB45.

"A Torrent of Election Day Disinformation is Coming. Here's How to Avoid Falling for It," Politico: https://www.politico.com/news/2024/11/05/election-day-disinformation-guide-00187343

"Rumors We've Fact-Checked About Voting, Results of 2024 Election," Snopes: https://www.snopes.com/collections/2024-election-rumors-voting-results/

"Misinformation and Competing Views of Reality Abounded Throughout 2020," Pew Research Center: https://www.pewresearch.org/journalism/2021/02/22/misinformation-and-competing-views-of-reality-abounded-throughout-2020/

"Misinformation is Eroding the Public's Confidence in Democracy," Brookings Institution: https://www.brookings.edu/articles/misinformation-is-eroding-the-publics-confidence-in-democracy/

"What Meta's New Studies Do—and Don't—Reveal About Social Media and Polarization," WIRED: https://www.wired.com/story/meta-social-media-polarization/

"TikTok's Role in U.S. and EU Elections," Pew Research Center: https://www.pewresearch.org/newsletter/the-briefing/the-briefing-2024-02-15/

"Donald Trump's Win Cements a New Era for Campaigning Online," WIRED: https://www.wired.com/story/donald-trump-online-campaign-era

"When Worldviews Collide: America's 2024 Election," Brookings Institution: https://www.brookings.edu/articles/when-worldviews-collide-americas-2024-election/

"Civic Engagement Strongly Tied to Local News Habits," Pew Research Center: https://www.pewresearch.org/journalism/2016/11/03/civic-engagement-strongly-tied-to-local-news-habits/

"Black US Voting 'Bloc' Composed of Five Distinct Political Groups, Survey Finds," The Guardian: https://www.theguardian.com/us-news/article/2024/sep/05/black-us-voting-bloc-survey.

Epilogue: Rewriting the Playbook of Modern Democracy

The 2024 presidential election was more than just a contest between two candidates; it was a referendum on the evolving dynamics of American democracy. At its core, the election reflected the changing tides of political engagement, campaign strategies, and voter expectations. From the silent majority's resurgence to the transformative role of grassroots activism, this election laid bare the forces shaping the nation's future.

Donald Trump's re-election was not just a testament to his campaign's mastery of targeted messaging, digital strategy, and emotional resonance but also a spotlight on the vulnerabilities within electoral systems, media narratives, and voter confidence. At the same time, Kamala Harris's campaign highlighted the challenges of connecting broad, systemic visions to the immediate concerns of a diverse electorate.

This book has explored the multifaceted lessons of 2024, uncovering critical truths about the intersection of strategy, media, and voter behavior. It has shown that while traditional tools like polling and financial resources still matter, they are no longer sufficient in an increasingly complex political arena. Instead, **adaptability, credibility, and connection** have emerged as the pillars of success in modern campaigns.

The Evolving Role of Media

Media bias and misinformation were central challenges in 2024, influencing voters' perceptions of candidates and policies. The speed at which misinformation spreads in the digital age demands vigilance and proactive solutions.

Media Literacy for Voters

Voters must develop the ability to discern credible sources from biased or manipulative content. Tools like the **CLEAR Model** provide a structured approach to evaluating media narratives, helping voters navigate conflicting information effectively.

Responsibility of Media Outlets

Media organizations must prioritize transparency, accuracy, and balance to rebuild trust. Journalism must rise above partisanship to be an unbiased arbiter of truth in this era.

Example: The Harris campaign was frequently misrepresented in viral social media posts that exaggerated her policy positions or fabricated controversies. Such distortions highlight the critical need for media literacy and accountability.

Grassroots Movements as Political Powerhouses

The 2024 election demonstrated that grassroots efforts are no longer supplemental—they are central to building trust, mobilizing voters, and shaping campaign narratives.

Empowering Local Voices: Campaigns can build lasting relationships with voters by prioritizing face-to-face interactions and addressing community-specific concerns.

Case Study: Trump's campaign in Pennsylvania leveraged local coalitions to amplify policies directly tied to regional industries. This targeted approach secured crucial support, showcasing the power of grassroots engagement.

The Importance of Data-Driven Precision

Digital tools like the **Digital Strategy Optimization Model (DSOM)** redefined how campaigns approach voter outreach. These tools enable campaigns to craft tailored messages and pivot based on voter sentiment in real-time.

Example: Trump's campaign used DSOM to adapt to emerging issues, such as rising inflation, ensuring that messaging aligned with voter priorities. This real-time adaptability gave his campaign a decisive edge.

The Need for Credibility and Trust

In an era of polarization and misinformation, credibility remains the cornerstone of successful campaigns. Voters demand leaders who align their promises with practical policies, delivering tangible results.

Transparency in Governance: Campaigns that foster trust through honesty and openness are better positioned to maintain voter loyalty beyond elections.

Looking Ahead: The Future of American Democracy

The lessons of 2024 extend beyond the mechanics of campaigning. They call on all stakeholders—candidates, voters, media outlets, and civic institutions—to adapt to the challenges of a rapidly evolving political landscape.

For Candidates and Campaigns

Future campaigns must embrace inclusivity, adaptability, and transparency. Success will depend on:

Understanding Voter Priorities

Campaigns must address immediate concerns while presenting a clear vision for the future.

Grassroots Engagement

Building meaningful connections at the local level fosters loyalty and trust.

Ethical Use of Digital Tools

Leveraging technology responsibly ensures credibility and prevents alienation.

For Voters

The electorate holds the power to shape the direction of democracy. To wield this power effectively, voters must:

Cultivate **media literacy** to navigate misinformation.

Critically evaluate candidates and policies, holding them accountable for their promises.

Actively participate in civic processes, ensuring that their voices are heard.

For Media Outlets

Media organizations must strike a balance between profitability and journalistic integrity. To regain public trust, they must:

Be transparent about editorial biases and funding sources.

Prioritize balanced reporting and diverse perspectives.

Foster a culture of accountability through public engagement.

For Civic Institutions

Organizations that promote voter education and engagement will play a pivotal role in sustaining democracy. By addressing systemic challenges such as voter suppression, misinformation, and electoral reform, these institutions ensure that democracy remains inclusive and resilient.

Closing Reflection: A Blueprint for Renewal

The 2024 election was not merely a historical moment but a reflection of America's strengths and weaknesses as a democracy. It highlighted the power of innovation, the resilience of grassroots movements, and the pressing need for systemic reform. Above all, it reminded us that democracy thrives when its citizens are informed, engaged, and united.

A Vision for the Future

The lessons of 2024 offer a roadmap for renewal. They challenge us to build bridges across divides, foster transparency and accountability, and create a political landscape where every voice matters. By embracing these principles, we can ensure that the next chapter of American democracy is defined not by division but by unity and progress.

Closing Thoughts

The future of democracy may not lie directly in the hands of a few but in the collective will of the many, though that will may be shaped and molded by the media gatekeepers. The message is to use that power to shape public opinion with a modicum of care to avoid the scenario that played out in November 2024 when the mainstream media appeared stunned to discover that they had misjudged entirely their campaign of influence over the public. That shock will continue to reverberate for some time and will serve as a lesson for future campaigns that play out in the media. In the meantime, as I had just finished watching the inauguration of the 47th President of the United States in the Rotunda at noon on January 20th, 2025, I wish Donald Trump a great second term!

How Trump Played the Media…Again

Gene Avakyan is a political newcomer but experienced in marketing, having established himself over nearly three decades as a technical leader and architect of numerous large-scale projects and marketing. He has worked with Los Angeles City Hall, including the Mayor's and City Attorney's offices, the Federal Aviation Administration, Deutsch Advertising, and dotcoms such as Zag, TrueCar, Spark Networks, and many others.

He earned a bachelor's degree in aerospace engineering from UCLA and an MBA from Pepperdine University. He founded VUGA Media Group (https://vugamediagroup.com), a media and PR company, and Edison Aerospace (https://edison.aero), a sustainable commercial agricultural aviation tech company.

www.ingramcontent.com/pod-product-compliance
Lightning Source LLC
Chambersburg PA
CBHW020538030426
42337CB00013B/904